THE BIG BOOK OF

SUPER MARIO

TRIUMPH
B O O K S

No part of this publication may be reproduced, stored in a retrieval system, or transmitted in any form by any means, electronic, mechanical, photocopying, or otherwise, without prior written permission of the publisher, Triumph Books LLC, 814 North Franklin Street; Chicago, Illinois 60610.

This book is available in quantity at special discounts for your group or organization.
For further information, contact:
Triumph Books LLC
814 North Franklin Street
Chicago, Illinois 60610
Phone: (312) 337-0747
www.triumphbooks.com

Printed in China
ISBN: 978-1-63727-121-6

Content packaged by Mojo Media, Inc.
Joe Funk: Editor
Jason Hinman: Creative Director
Jack Hinman: Game Master

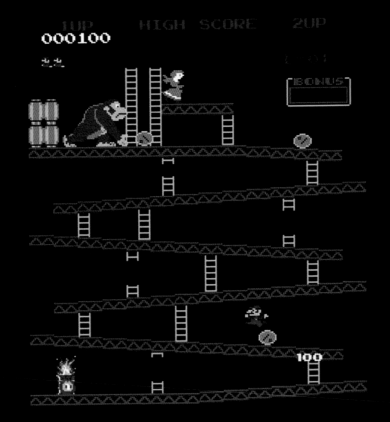

CONTENTS

INTRODUCTION

MARIO
001300   ⊕×01   WORLD
1-1

200

Mario has been around for years, starting out in the early 80's. Everyone thought that this little character had real promise. The creators had him in a different game originally, but soon gave him his own game because everyone loved the little guy.

Mario is now one of the biggest characters of all time, but the game makers with Nintendo didn't know that when they put him in Donkey Kong. They just felt that this little tradesman had a role to play in the world taken over by the massive gorilla.

Having appeared in over 200 video games since he was created, he has gained a lot of fame throughout the Nintendo world and still continues to have not only games of his own, but also movies, shows and much more that feature him and his brother Luigi.

One of the biggest and best selling franchises of all time, Mario has gone to the top of the charts with many of his games and even some he's featured in as well. Super Mario set the scene for him, but then came his other signature games such as Mario Kart, Mario's Time Machine, Mario Tennis and so many more.

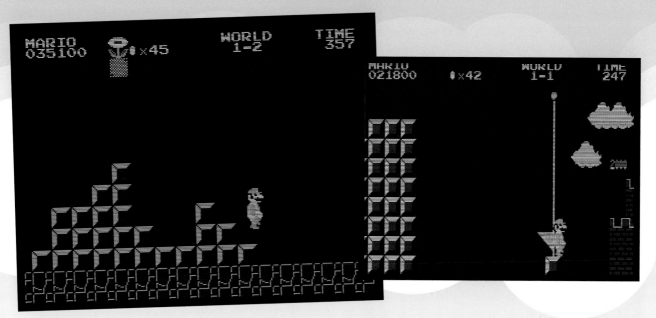

With all the games out there, Mario continues to be a loved character for so many. Players looking for quality games with a character they know well, instinctively turn toward Mario titles, and he continues to be a favorite for many.

NINTENDO'S BEGINNINGS

Nintendo wasn't always just a video and game console maker for players. The company started small as a trading card platform, helping players trade and play, and as a toy maker. They didn't dive into the game console business until many of the consoles became bigger and more well known.

With this new technology, the group that was working inside a tiny office space, then developed not only a new game but a new system. This led to the evolution of Nintendo itself. It was something that would make them much bigger than Pac Man, as well as any of the other game makers out there.

To this day Nintendo continues to top the charts with their games and game consoles. Many of which are currently handheld, making a big impact on the way that gaming is done today.

They're the gaming systems you know and use currently.

MARIO'S CREATION

Mario had a humble beginning as a side-story character for the hit game Donkey Kong. The makers had no idea Mario would go as far as he did. Donkey Kong was one of the first ambitious game projects by Nintendo that the creators hoped would become as big as Pac Man.

While Donkey Kong did make it quite big, he wasn't able to beat out that mega-successful dot eating character.

As the creators realized how popular Mario was, they decided to give him a name, give him a background and then present him in a new game, a game all his own, that people could really enjoy.

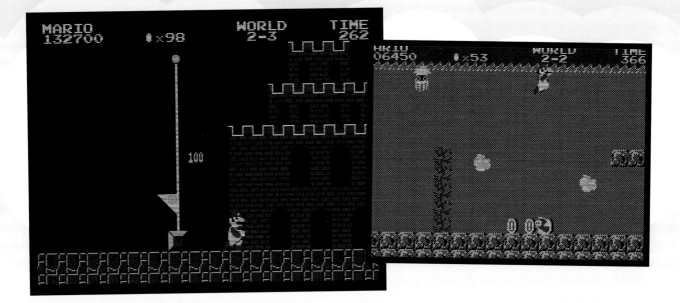

Naming the character also gave a face and a purpose to the little pixelated guy. After a bit of a debate the creators settled on Mario as his name, but head creator Shigeru Miyamoto almost went with Mr. Video instead. If the makers had given him a name like Mr. Video, he wouldn't have made it very far. He was supposed to be personable and someone that would provide hours of fun much like a friend. A name like Mr. Video just doesn't match his theme which is why it's fortunate for Nintendo that they ended up going with Mario as the name, because they've enjoyed great success from the little jumping guy.

Over time Mario has grown and evolved. He has become better looking due to the evolution of game systems and the way the characters and items on the screen look.

Learn more about the history of Mario and how he became as big as he is today. It won't come as a shock to know that he has a much deeper history than most people realize.

You might not have even realized that Mario has been around as long as he has, or that he's evolved so much. Your parents might have even played the original Mario games when they were younger, so ask them about how he was then, as compared to how he is now.

SUPER MARIO BROS. TAKE THE STAGE

Of course, you're very familiar with Mario, but what about his brother Luigi? He didn't make his big entrance until some time later to provide a little more character diversification.

With Mario Bros. coming out big and in full force, many people thought that Mario's full name was Mario Bros. Nintendo finally released to the audience that Mario's name is actually Mario Mario, and that the "Brothers" was just the name of the game that also included Luigi in it.

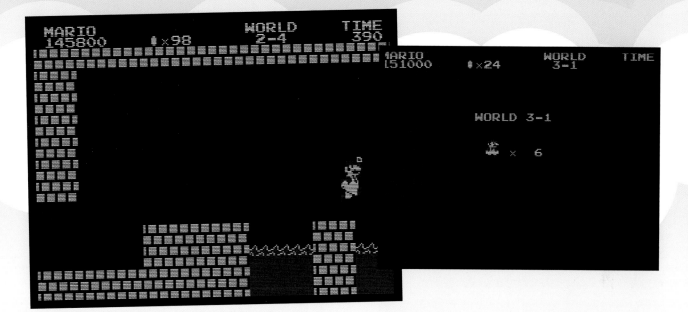

Of course, Luigi is now featured in almost every game that comes out with Mario, but he never was in the beginning. He didn't come out until 1983, a few years after Mario had already been created and introduced to the world.

When you think of Super Mario Bros. games as they are today, you're allowed to choose which character you'd like to play throughout the game, whether it is Mario, Luigi, Princess Toadstool or any of the others. That wasn't always the case though.

It's a bit shocking to find out you once were stuck just playing Mario. Read on to learn how the games have evolved over the years and become richer with features.

What's your favorite thing about Mario? Do you have a favorite game that he is featured in? Have you played the newest Mario game that's recently been released for Nintendo Switch?

Now's the time to learn all about Mario and what the little lovable character has to offer, from the beginning of his creation onward. He's been in countless games that we know and love, and is one of the biggest video game icons today.

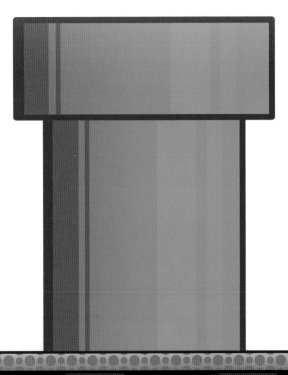

THE BEGINNING

Mario didn't always have the spotlight in his own games. He started off in a much humbler way than many characters do. While most new characters are given their own games in the beginning, Mario was just a side character that had to grow into the fully-fledged feature character that he is today.

Mario had to win our hearts over time, and that's probably part of the reason that he's such a well-developed character today.

He started out in the early 80's as a side character in the game, Donkey Kong.

As an Italian plumber, no one thought he would go very far in the world of video games. However, with some time, he has become one of the most recognizable characters throughout the world. He is featured in over 100 video games and it's hard to imagine a world without Mario in it.

However, many people want to know where he came from. **What is Mario's story?**

The struggling toy and card shop known as Nintendo wanted to enter into the world of video games. Somewhat new to the market, these games seemed to make an impact on the world. They wanted to get into the action by creating a character that would make a difference.

They started off in the world of video games working on arcade game creations. These pixelated games meant for the public weren't as involved or developed as the games we all know today.

They tried out a few early games but to no avail, nothing stuck with the audiences that they were trying to reach. Radar Scope, one of their first games barely sold at all. This left the company with a difficult challenge to overcome, they had to find a game that would make an impact in the gaming world. A game that would make Nintendo into a recognizable brand to gamers.

To help kickstart this dream, the company approached artist Shigeru Miyamoto. They asked him to design a game for the company, hoping that his skills with game creation would lead to a game that would sell out and hopefully bring in something for the small company.

Not a programmer, Miyamoto had to think out a story line before even being able to put together graphics that would fit into a playable game. That's something that didn't happen at the time. Creators would throw together games and work on the story line and extras as they go as more of an afterthought than anything else. As you can guess, Miyamoto's early games were a smash success. He started off with Donkey Kong, but he built a bunch of other successes as well.

Miyamoto went on to create some of the well known games of your childhood, such as Legend of Zelda, Pikmin, Star Fox and even the Wii Sports bundle that comes with the console. He continues to work for Nintendo and is a big name within the industry.

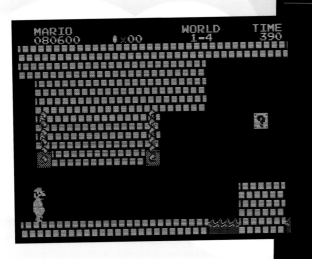

THE BIRTH OF DONKEY KONG

Hiring Miyamoto led to the creation of the game, Donkey Kong. This was a game between a gorilla, a girlfriend and a man. It was not only something that many of the producers didn't think would go far, but it was far from the video games that we know now.

Even though Mario at that time was known as "Jump Man," he still made headlines in the game. Many people wanted to see more of him. Back then, the character was only able to jump up and down, go side to side and climb ladders. With the evolution of gaming systems in the future, that quickly changed though.

Donkey Kong quickly became a fast seller in the gaming industry and all because the game makers decided to move forward with a different type of game. They created something that made headlines because the characters were more developed and had a story line.

Donkey Kong quickly became a mainstay in arcades around the world, and everyone was able to try their luck rescuing the fair maiden.

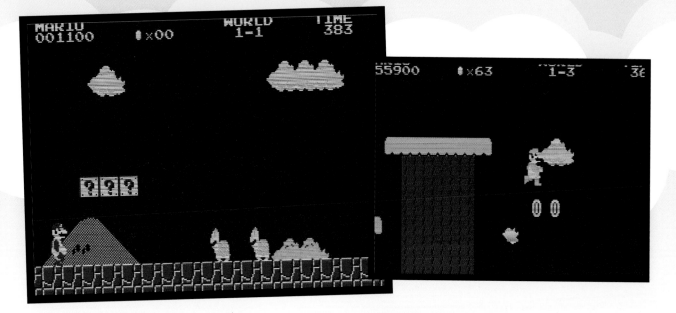

WHERE MARIO GOT HIS NAME

Everyone always asks where Mario's name came from. It's a seemingly random name, but it's one that definitely has a back story to it and it's something that is pretty interesting.

When the team had to come up with a new game after Donkey Kong made it big, they wanted to feature little Jump Man in the game. However, with a name like Jump Man, it just wasn't going to make the impact that they wanted.

While brain storming in their small office, they were thinking of game ideas and names for this little guy. The office owner then came in and demanded that he get rent money for the office space that they were using.

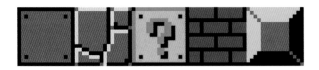

Working on getting a game out there and distributed, the landlord made a big scene while demanding the late rent money. His name? Mario. The staff members then started joking and calling the little Jump Man, Mario. He looked somewhat the same, had the same overalls and the same appearance, so to this day, that's how Mario is known.

As for the landlord, he'd rather no one knew that the little character was actually named after him.

Additionally, they wanted the character to be seen as a hard worker within the industry. He needed to do a trade job that he was dedicated to. This led the developers to create him as a plumber, instead of just a general handyman that was once shown in the Donkey Kong arcade game.

This put not only a name to the character, but also a back story for him, as well. It's something that wasn't normally done in the past but the creators felt it was necessary in order to make a connection with the players.

MOVING ON TO DIFFERENT GAMES

Since Mario was developed, the makers wanted to make a game of his own. They wanted to show the world that he was here and ready to stay for more play. With so many ideas going through the team, they had to come up with something that was not like any of the other games out there, including Donkey Kong.

He was a 'go-to' character, which put him in any spot needed, which was ideal for many different types of games that they could create focused around Mario.

The first game that featured Mario as the lead was Mario Bros., a game where Luigi was also introduced into the story line. However, before Mario Bros. came out, Donkey Kong Junior let the world know that little Jump Man was actually named Mario before he had a chance to get his own game.

This brought in a lot of attention to the Mario Bros. game that would soon hit the shelves and then sell out fairly quickly.

Read through the following chapters to learn more about the Mario games that would soon follow throughout the years. Jump Man started it all for Nintendo in Donkey Kong, but soon made a wave in the gaming world with many other appearances and all the games that he was placed in.

He was even featured in movies over the years. Find out where the Mario you know now came from and read more about his past and development by Nintendo creators, themselves.

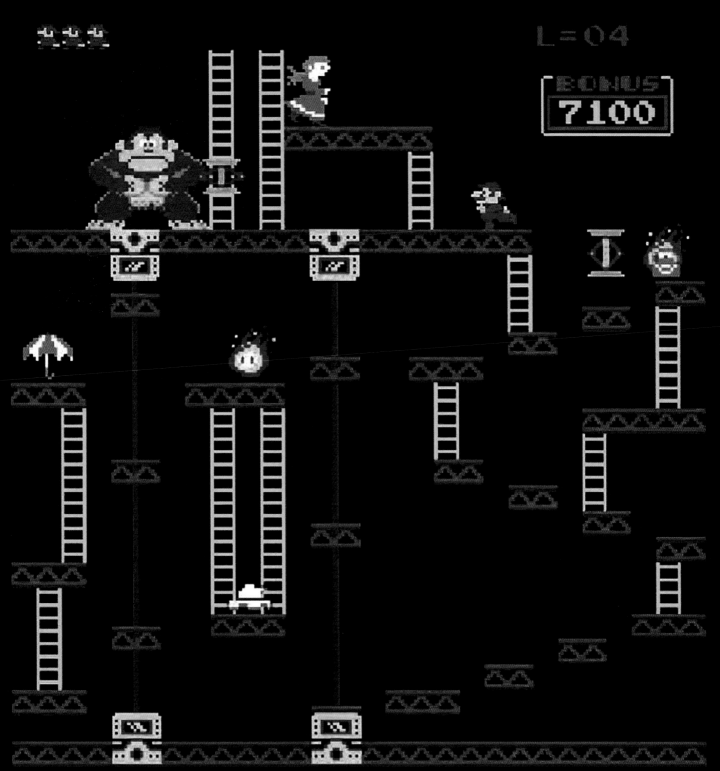

070400   070400

L=04

BONUS
7100

MARIO OF THE 1980s

Mario started his early years known as 'Jump Man.' After a nice little makeover, he then was given the name Mario. This change gave him more graphical development and also made him into a more complex character. It allowed him to be seen throughout an ever expanding and growing world of games.

The little guy was a big hit in the Donkey Kong games, which led developers to believe he would be ideal for a standalone set of games. This was an idea much of the rest of the world didn't agree with, they were proven wrong in a big way though. They quickly found out that Mario's debut would be a giant hit.

Mario started off big and only got bigger over the years. He continues to come out in new games ever few years and has been featured on different game systems throughout the history of Nintendo. Read on for more in-depth information about Mario's past and what made him into the rich and well-known hit character he is today.

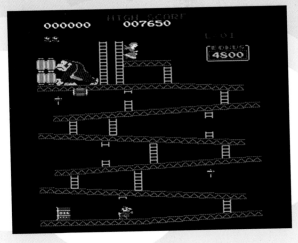

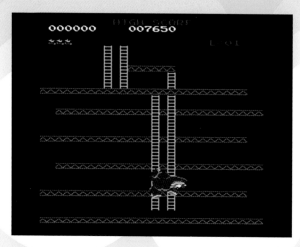

PIXELATED AND NOT WELL KNOWN

Starting out as just a pixelated character, Jump Man was featured in the Donkey Kong games. He was only able to move in small directions and climb ladders. This was something that needed improvement, but since he wasn't the star of the game, they didn't focus all of their attention on just Jump Man. Donkey Kong was the real star of the show that the creators felt that they needed to focus on.

However, after seeing how he was adored, Donkey Kong creators knew that Jump Man could have a real future, but in his own game world developed around him.

It didn't take long after this realization for Mario to become a hit success. Creators of the game put out the original, and quickly launched a whole succession of sequels building on Mario's success.

CHANGING HIS SPRITE

Enhancements were made on Mario's sprite to make him stand out on the new NES system. This was developed in 1981. This made Mario have a better look, a clear focus in the game and provide the player with better graphics overall. The NES system was designed to revolutionize gaming for players and create a graphically superior experience.

With every game thereafter, Mario kept changing his look. He'd become more focused as a person and less pixelated. His outfits would stand out more and he would have more detail.

Almost every Mario that came out would soon become something clearer and different. This was the wave of a new gaming era for those that would soon be playing on the new Nintendo systems with Mario at their side.

DID YOU KNOW?

Mario was once just a square pixelated box and they were unable to create hair that did not look funny, which is why Mario is wearing a hat in every game that he is shown in, especially the games from the past.

Mario's look has changed so often that sometimes the early Mario characters are known as Mario's dark times. This is because the little guy on the original games looks nothing like the full-fledged character that we're all so familiar with today.

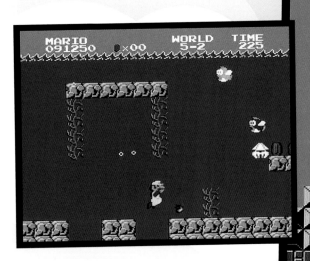

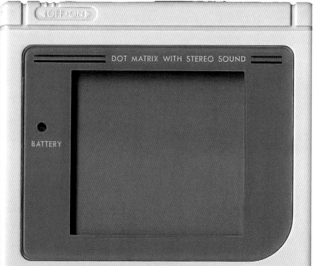

THE CONSOLES OF THE 80'S

The Nintendo Entertainment System (NES) was the first ever home gaming system that would feature Mario and his friends. This system was much different from the arcade games where the games would have to be played and were normally in public areas not in homes of the players. This system was released in 1983, allowing for those that loved Mario to bring the action from the arcade to their home.

The Nintendo Game Boy was the next device to come out and provide users with a way to play Mario on the go. Sure it was large, and ate batteries with a huge appetite, but the cool new device allowed players to bring the fun with them on black and white screens with pixelated characters everywhere. The Game Boy came out in 1989 and the makers of Mario would have to find ways to create a game that would transfer from the NES to the Game Boy system without an issue.

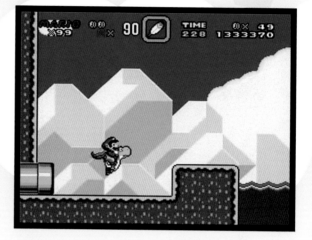

WE WELCOME MARIO BROS.

Times changed for Mario after his initial release and in 1983, Mario Bros. was established. This was an arcade-style game where you could play on your own or 1v1 against your brother Luigi. Of course, while playing alone, you had to go through the two tier, 2 pipe, turtle and mushroom infested level all on your own. This was a challenge that many gamers accepted.

A lot of players from this time would fixate on the game, because it was revolutionary for its time. There were many obstacles and challenges other games simply didn't have back then. The uniqueness of Mario Bros. was

mostly due to the creators with Nintendo creating a story line, instead of throwing items together and calling it a game like many other creators during that time period.

This was the first game where Mario is known to be a plumber, and also the game that welcomes his brother Luigi to the game. It was also the first game where Mario was the main character and not Jump Man that was featured in a Donkey Kong game, though he was Mario in Donkey Kong Junior that had released a year earlier.

SUPER MARIO BROS. FOLLOWS

Two years later, every player was excited to see a new game evolve with Mario, Super Mario Bros. This was the first game where Mario had to rescue a princess in distress. Bowser was also featured in this version of Mario. Many new characters, faces, items and obstacles were then presented. Not only that, but Mario ended up going through quite the makeover to get here. This was to keep up with the new graphics of the gaming system, which made a huge difference on the way that Mario was presented throughout the game.

Super Mario Bros. 2 was released shortly after the first. The first had done so well, the makers wanted to release another. The second version was released in 1988, followed by a third version. Super Mario Bros. 3 sold out more copies than other console games throughout the entire world. This was in 1989, when the game makers were slowing production of games, but would soon come up with another Mario game to send out to the world.

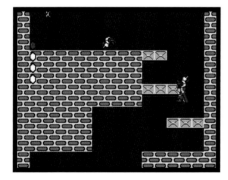

DID YOU KNOW?

Super Mario Bros. 2 was not originally a Super Mario Bros. game. It was known as Doki Doki Panic. Replacing the original characters of the game with Super Mario Bros. characters, it became a Mario game.

This is the only Mario game to feature Wart as a main boss. It also gives players the opportunity to be other Mario characters, not just Mario or Luigi.

In both of these games, the player's main goal is to help Mario track down the princess, defeat the bosses and in the later versions they can even play as any of the Mario characters that they would like to be. These games brought more variation to the table, allowing the players to have a bit more control.

With even more features to the game, this quickly became a popular choice for many people out there searching for a game that would deliver. All three versions of Super Mario were able to do just that and keep someone occupied for hours.

Even today the original Super Mario Bros. games are ported to the latest Nintendo game consoles. They've been redone again and again and still remain as one of the most beloved of all the Nintendo games ever released. Mario is one of the most original Nintendo games and will remain as one of the favorites even if Nintendo stops releasing the games.

SUPER MARIO LAND TOWARDS THE END

Nearing the end of the 80's, Super Mario Land was the one that bid the 80's goodbye. The game features a more detailed sprite to play with. This gave a clearer picture and some think, better game play.

DID YOU KNOW?

Power ups during the 80's weren't something that Mario had access to. You had to use Mario's regular abilities to beat the obstacles and the bosses that stood in your way. There weren't any special mushrooms to make you grow, or spring blocks to help you jump higher while playing through the levels.

Super Mario Land gave Mario a more friendly look thanks to the increase in detail, and he took on a less sharp look and become a more lovable character as a result. This was a problem that the Game Boy Mario games were struggling with though. The limitations made it hard to give Mario all of the graphics they wanted to. The sprite that they created just wouldn't transfer from system to system well, so they had to come up with a better character creation for those that wanted Mario on a handheld Nintendo system.

Super Mario Land was a game that welcomed you to the world of Mario. With mushrooms, levels to beat and many obstacles that stood in your way, the players would have to make it through the land, beat the obstacles and the bosses and then rescue the princess. Thought of as just a regular guy, he didn't start getting many super powers until later on during the game development phase.

The next wave of Mario games is when the power-ups were first introduced. It's also when there were new focuses that would make the games go even further than they already have, with more objectives and complex level designs. This made a difference in the world of Mario and what was to follow.

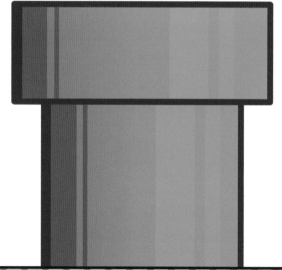

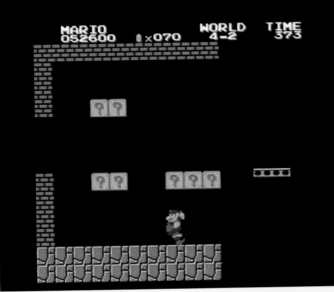

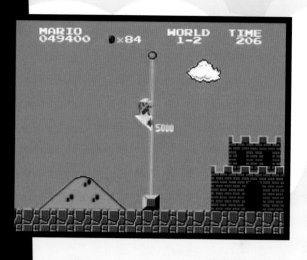

Though quite pixelated and not as smooth as the gaming consoles that you currently play on, Mario captured the hearts of gamers all over the world before personal gaming consoles even existed. That's pretty impressive if you ask us, and it's the reason that Mario has been able to persist as such a lovable character for all these years.

Mario continued on throughout the 90's showing up in a whole slew of games. The little plumber was the main character of many of these games, but also showed up as a side character in some as well. Keep reading to learn more about the 90's and Mario that would take over the world ahead.

Each of the games had its own challenges that kept players captivated, but with major advancements with each new gaming platform, the industry would continue to evolve the lovable character that everyone knows as Mario today.

As the 90's came, the 80's Mario quickly became outdated. Developers needed to act to keep the little guy fresh, interesting and something that players from future generations would want to experience. This led them to create new games, with more exciting objectives and to also make a new character that would change the face of Mario on TV screens all across the world.

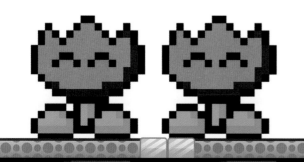

MARIO OF THE 1990s

Moving Mario to the 90's was no easy task for the original developers. He had to be changed significantly to help him blend in with the new game-rich atmosphere with more capable game systems and better graphics. During this period of continual upgrades Mario became more detailed and better looking, but also came up against a whole new set of obstacles with new powers at his disposal. The 90's were a serious period of evolution for Mario, and the time that most features we know and love today came to be.

NINTENDO⁶⁴

Walk with us and find out even more about gaming systems of the 90's and also the Mario games that were released to the public. These are more closely related to the Mario games that you know currently, making them a bit more relatable and fun.

GAMING CONSOLES OF THE 90'S

Gaming consoles were plentiful in the 90's, and with those consoles came a whole new breed of characters, story lines and original games. Mario was among that mix of games and offered gaming entertainment in a big way for Nintendo.

The Super Nintendo Entertainment System (SNES) was one of the systems that bounced off of the original NES system developed in the 80's. It brought better graphics and smoother gameplay than the original. This made a huge difference in how many of the games, including Mario, were played on the system. The SNES was released in 1990, just in time to take the 90's by storm!

The Nintendo 64 was the next in line for Nintendo, and it was a revolutionary system with a built-in joystick and up to four players at a time on one screen. It was a huge upgrade that came out in 1996 and with it a whole new generation of Donkey Kong and Mario games as well. They were more widely available than ever before. The N64 was a gaming system that everyone had to have and it offered a whole collection of cool games, such as Star Fox, Metroid Prime, Zelda and others that were not Mario related.

The Game Boy Color and Game Boy Pocket both came out towards the end of the 90's. The Color was in 1998 and the Pocket 1996. Both these systems allowed the user to play the games they wanted while on the go. The Game Boy Pocket didn't have color, but had clear graphics as compared to the original Game Boy. The Color was able to provide clearer graphics, that were also in color, which is something that was very big at the time.

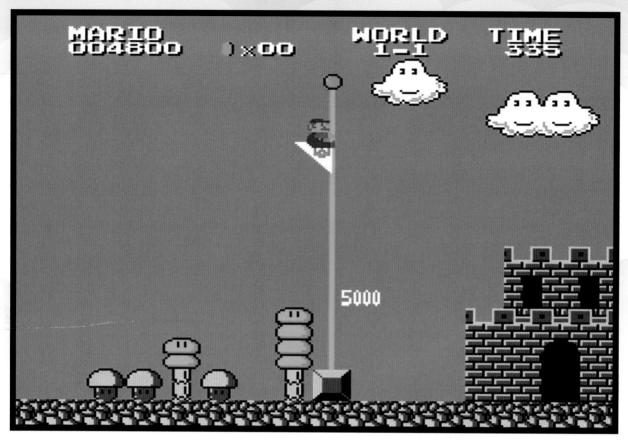

There were many Mario games that could be played and that came out during the 90's. Take a look at some of the biggest Mario games to be released in the 90's.

MARIO'S SPRITES CHANGED AGAIN

Mario's been evolving since the little guy served as Jump Man back in the early 80's, but the 90's were an especially exciting period for Mario. He became more colorful, more detailed and stopped looking like a little square and more like a little man. The developers found ways to make the games more enjoyable and life-like and that was a big deal for Mario fans.

Mario's sprite took on a different appearance. To create a more cartoon-like appearance, developers made use of the larger color palette available with new more powerful systems. Mario started to look more like a cartoon character you'd see on television and not one that was pixelated.

This was one of the largest differences that Mario of the 90's had to offer versus the little pixelated block man of the 80's. Mario had smoother graphics, better gameplay overall and definitely had more details than the previous versions.

SUPER MARIO WORLD

This is the first Mario game to ever be launched for Super Nintendo in 1991, but it was still a hit nonetheless. Princess Toadstool was once again kidnapped and the savvy Mario had to come out and defeat the bosses in order to save her from certain doom. The backdrop is in Dinosaur Land with many different playable zones, giving the player the control of where they'd like to play.

Some of the new lands that the players were able to take on included Yoshi's Island, Bridges, Star Land, Donut Plains, Vanilla Dome, Chocolate Island, Forest of Illusion and the Valley of Bowser, as well as a few others. This is also where you get to meet the newest Yoshi characters that come out more in the next few games.

One of the newest features for this game is the scrollable World Map, which wasn't in the previous games and gave users more control over their playing capabilities.

SUPER MARIO KART

Still a popular game today, Super Mario Kart has actually been around since 1992. This was the first ever racing game that was presented by Super Mario and it was one that quickly took off because all of the characters from the Super Mario games were featured in the racing.

Three different cups were proposed as the winning trophies for those that came in to take the lead. You could get the Mushroom, Flower and Star. Some even got to unlock a fourth trophy known as the Special Cup. The developers also added three different racing speeds and three different modes for those that wanted a bit more control over the racing as well as their playing experience levels.

One of the coolest parts of this racing game, besides that it was racing, was that the player could also choose the character that they wanted to speed with. All of the favorite Mario characters were there, such as Yoshi, Mario, Luigi, Donkey Kong Jr., Toad and even Bowser.

The sprites and karts in this racing game were not as advanced as more modern-day Mario Kart games, but they still were much better than the 80's Mario that so many have played with in the past.

SUPER MARIO RPG

Role Playing Games became more popular throughout the world, which meant that Mario had to step it up a bit and come out with a new game that he could be featured in, with a complete story line. Coming out in 1996, Mario again took a turn to a new game and came with a new look.

Breaking away from the 2D track that so many have been playing before, a new wave of character came and went for this new game. Partnering with SquareSoft, Nintendo set out to make a new host of sprites to use in the game that would come with more 3D qualities.

The first ever Mario RPG game had a whole new story line and it was released in Europe, where RPG games were becoming one of the biggest growing games in the industry.

MARIO GOING TOWARDS 3D

Mario has always had 2D capabilities and appearance. This is how the systems worked in the 80's and part of the 90's, and how they could render the graphics so smoothly. However, with the change in technology and the growing world around us, the need for a 3D model became greater. While, he didn't completely go 3D, the new 2.25D gave Mario more dimension than he has ever had.

The new look was found in the Super Mario RPG: Legend of the Seven Stars for the Super Nintendo and then following with Wrecking Crew for the same system in 1998. This changed the way he looked, even if the previous games for the system still gave him a 2D appearance.

SUPER MARIO 64

First released in 1996 for the Nintendo 64 gaming console, Super Mario 64 put Mario back out there and brought him back to life after not being seen for a bit. This game gave players more, allowing them to try a whole new level with a more immersive world. Battling Bowser throughout different lands, Mario has to work to save Princess Peach this time.

Princess Peach is imprisoned and Mario has to go through over 100 star worlds in order to get to her and free her from the clutches of Bowser. He saves a new person with each level, getting him closer to the end of the game with each save that he makes. The levels do get a bit harder as you go along, but the main focus is to just get to Peach and be able to save her from the prison before it's too late.

With each new save, Mario collects power ups, hints, tricks and more from the appreciation of those that he saves. This early world not only showed that the gaming systems could handle larger, more intricate games but it also served as a template for a new world in the future of all Mario games.

While this is much different from the original games, it still had many of the qualities and characters that you would expect from a Mario game. It still ends with the appreciation of Princess Peach once he rescues her from Bowser.

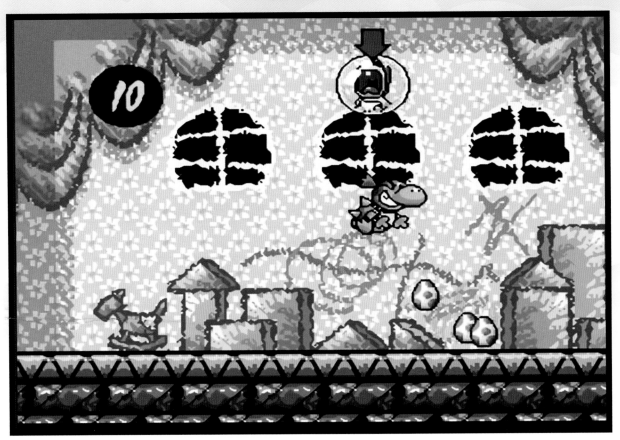

SUPER MARIO LAND 2

Originally released for the Game Boy systems, this game was a pocket version that allowed those that loved the first Super Mario Land that came out in 1989 to enjoy a second, more updated version. The game came out in 1992, making it one of the early Mario games from the 90's. Sometimes known as 6 Golden Coins, Mario had new obstacles to overcome in the battle.

Mario's evil twin Wario has raged against the world and Mario has to try to stop him before any more damage is done. He placed an evil spell across all of Mario Land and now the residents of the area think that Wario is the master and Mario is their enemy. This is a pretty different plot, but it is one that plays off of the original Super Mario Land.

In order to stop Wario and his evil plans, Mario has to find 6 Golden Coins that are hidden throughout each of the levels that the players have to play through. This will help him not only gain access back into his castle, but also break the spell and beat Wario. A bit different from the other games, but still just as fascinating. You have to be Mario and race against time to find all the hidden coins.

SUPER MARIO WORLD 2: YOSHI'S ISLAND

Released in 1995, this game made a storm within the Mario world by introducing the little Yoshi and background of where he came from. Starting out as a baby, both Luigi and Mario are carried by a stork over the sea. However, Luigi is then stolen by Magikoopa Kamek and Mario has to fight his way to find his brother.

Dropped off at Yoshi's Island, home to the Yoshis, Mario has to become friends with these creatures and find a way to make it back to his brother before something bad happens to him. Journey through all of the levels and worlds of the game with the Yoshis by your side. Just a baby yourself, you have to go rescue baby Luigi from Kamek and Bowser, who are also both babies.

This was a different story line than the others, but it provided a new world for players and also a different story line they had to follow along with. This is where many of the Yoshis and their background came about, so you're able to get an idea of where the Yoshis all come from when you play this game.

The 90's brought a lot to the table in the world of Mario. With so many things happening at once, it was a great period to be a Mario fan.

Characters and story lines were continually changing and the games in the 90's gave fans more information about Mario and the other characters and the world they belong to.

Current Mario games continue to change and adapt with the new systems and technology, but these were a huge part of childhood for so many children. Mario continued his evolution over the years, becoming more complex and advanced to match the improving game systems.

Learn more about Mario and what the 2000's brought for him and systems that came out during those years. The Mario of yesterday is evolving more and more to be like the Mario that we know and love today.

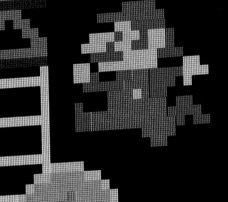

SCORE

7650

L=0

BO

35

MARIO OF THE 2000s

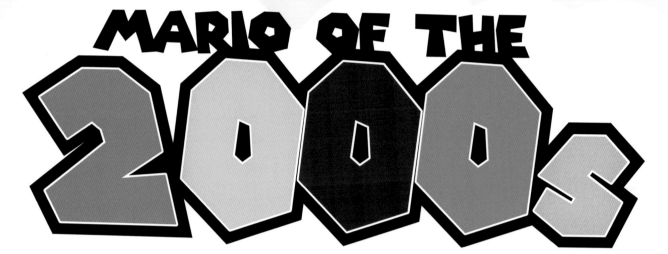

Mario went on to expand his reach into different areas and gaming systems in the 2000's. His sprite also changed with him. Those cartoon characters started being more detailed, while also being able to do more within the games, since the technology of the time improved, the 2000's brought a lot of benefits to those that wanted a bit more Mario in their lives.

Learn more about the Mario that started your generation and see where it has led us to this day. You may be surprised to know that he has come a very long way in the 2000's to get to the games that he is in now.

THE GAMING CONSOLES OF THE 2000'S

With the 2000's brought a new wave of gaming systems. This meant for better gaming experiences for everyone that wanted enjoy something greater. With better graphics and smooth story lines, these systems easily took the world by storm.

The Game Boy Advance made a wave in the world of handheld devices. Coming to the market in 2001, many people wanted to grab one of these more advanced handheld devices. They provided a way to bring the game to wherever you go, but also had colorful games that allowed you to play easily. Of course, there were many versions such as the SP or Micro that were later released, but each followed the same general concept of the Advance.

Another handheld console that hit the market was the Nintendo DS. It hit the market in 2004, with many more models to follow in the next few years after. The DS was also a big hit and provided users with a way to interact more intuitively by tapping or touching the bottom screen, while also using the top for viewing the games. Many of the DS versions soon followed after the original, such as the Lite and the DSi.

The Nintendo Game Cube came out in 2001, as a home gaming console following the N64. This also gained a lot of attention in the market since it supplied gamers with not only new games, but better graphics. The Game Cube was an updated version of the 64 that everyone wanted to have in their homes.

The Wii was another Nintendo game system that was released in the 2000's, coming out in 2006. This flew off the shelves at full force. It was a game system that allowed you to interact with the games that were in the console. It came with controllers much different from the normal game pads and paddles that gamers were used to using. It was an innovation in the gaming field that many other game makers had not yet reached.

MARIO'S SPRITE CHANGED FORM

With new game systems and new games came new looks for Mario that was once a little box guy with a hat and overalls. With so much more powerful machines capable of better graphics, the once hard to see character on the screen was now fully detailed and easily noticed within each of the games that he made an appearance on.

This was pretty much where the character stayed throughout the years. He has had some better graphics within the games, but overall, he is still the same Italian guy with a red hat, blue overalls and gloves. The mustache is here to stay as well, so check for it in any of the games that you come across.

SUPER MARIO SUNSHINE

The next major Mario game that was released and accepted throughout the USA was designed for the Game Cube. Initially, the game took a lot of backlash because the controller for the system did not work as well as the players had hoped it would, but with time, it ended up drawing people to the originality and need to learn something brand new.

Super Mario Sunshine was a novelty for Mario fans because it was different than what they were used to from Mario games. It forced fans to learn a new controller, and also to learn how to navigate an entirely new world.

This game also welcomes another bad version of Mario to it, Shadow Mario. Set to pollute the entire island where Mario and his friends are taking a vacation, Shadow Mario must be defeated in order to save the island and also the people that live on it. Mario is arrested for the crimes that Shadow Mario commits since they look the same, and that's how the game starts off.

One of the biggest additions to this game which wasn't shown in previous Mario games is the FLUDD. It is used to propel Mario into the air, promote cleanup on the island and

even work as an offensive tool if needed. Invented by Professor E. Gadd, he is able to use this tool for many different tasks that he comes across. Bowser Jr. is who Mario meets in the cleanup process.

Beat Bowser and be able to enjoy the rest of your vacation again once you collect Princess Peach, since he took her back with him to the castle. While there, the paintbrushes that the professor needs need to be collected. Many objectives and obstacles stand in your way, but this makes this Mario game much more enjoyable than older versions.

NEW SUPER MARIO BROS.

The New Super Mario Bros. was made to mimic the look and feel that the original Super Mario Bros. came out with. Much different from the other games on the market, this was meant to have that classic appeal but also have new upgrades that players already knew and loved when it came to playing Mario.

Bowser Jr. is back in this game and better than ever. He is ready to grab Princess Peach and hit the road again when it comes to taking her from Mario. Of course, he does and then Mario has to go through quests in eight different worlds to find her once again. Blending all of the old styles with the new, this was a game that hit the shelves hard and was able to deliver to those Mario fans!

SUPER MARIO GALAXY

Bringing together everything spacey, you're going to want to try out Mario in space with this awesome game. It was released in 2007, and a lot of those that love Mario wanted to follow along with this all new Mario game concept.

One of the most noted aspects of this Mario game was that it took a completely new direction. Bowser is of course in this one, but he made his castle go up in space, so it is out of reach for Mario to rescue the princess. Mario has to then travel through space and collect Power Stars in order to reach the princess. It is a bit different from the normal games, but definitely interesting.

nection between recent graffiti inciden

With new puzzles and abilities, Mario could do much more than on some of the other Mario games out there. The game was a fresh take on the Mario franchise and many of the regular players loved the new feel. Super Mario Galaxy 2 was then presented shortly after the first. Bowser is seen as a giant in this one, Mario gets a spaceship and Princess Peach is kidnapped yet again. It is a regular Mario theme that has stood strong for so many years.

With the changes made throughout the years to Mario, you can expect that 2010 to this present day is going to bring its own exciting flavor of Mario games with it. The next chapter is all the Mario games you know and love recently.

Walk with us and find out exactly what you can expect from the excitement that awaits you within the kingdom! Are you ready to rescue Princess Peach again?

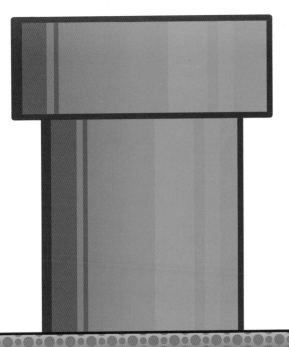

MARIO OF THE 2010s

Mario has come and gone and changed in so many ways that those that were around when the first Mario came out are surprised by what the games now look like. With the changing games over time, Mario has definitely gotten more abilities, jumps to new heights (literally) and can now take on the bad guys that come to try and defeat him in new and exciting ways, even if it is mostly just Bowser.

Now you can rescue the princess in many different levels, modes and game backdrops. This is something that a lot of the Mario players of the world love to do today. If you're searching for a little bit more fun with Mario and his gang, then follow us and let us show you the coolest Mario-based features and games to come out between 2010 and today!

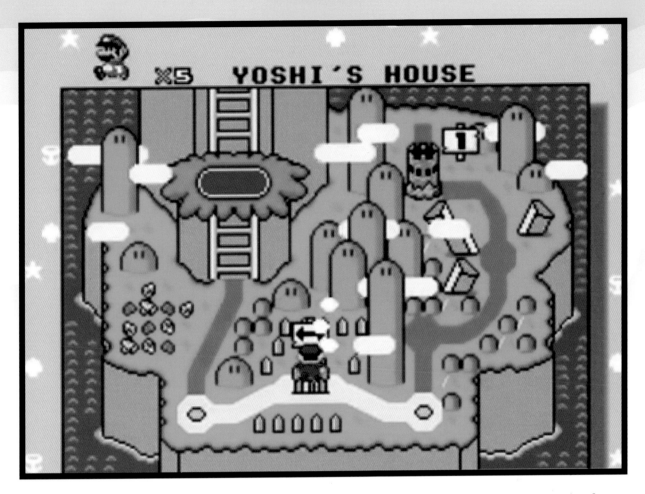

GAMING CONSOLES YOU ALL KNOW WELL

The consoles of this time didn't change too much compared to what was offered in the 2000's, they're basically more powerful systems with some cool new features added here and there. These consoles are perfect when it comes to playing a little Mario, just don't forget to throw in a little Star Fox every now and again too.

The Wii U was one of the biggest gaming consoles to hit the market after the Wii and almost everyone wanted one of these systems to play on. Providing the user with a way to play the Wii on your television screen like normal, but also the ability to pull it away from the screen using the large tablet controller, the game is right there in front of you even if someone else wants to use the television! Much like a small computer, this console is very different from the newer Xbox One and Playstation 4 released just a short while after the WiiU.

The Nintendo Switch is the next console after the Wii U and it's an even more novel concept entirely. It provides the user with a way to play right at home off the television or to bring the gaming with them wherever they go. One of the biggest advances throughout the gaming world, it's a console that gamers are lining up to get, especially the hardcore Nintendo fans out there. The system relies on a single portable system that connects to a television base for full-sized viewing at home, or slips out and accepts controllers at either side to create a gaming tablet for on-the-go. Easily switch between playing on the television and on the tablet-like device on-the-fly, making it easy to keep gaming no matter where you go.

MARIO'S SPRITE MADE A LEAP AND BOUND

Mario's sprite did not change too much between the 2000's to the 2010's. He might seem a bit different in each of the games that are presented throughout the years, but that is just dependent on the theme of the game, overall he still is around the same in terms of details.

NEW SUPER MARIO BROS. 2

Just like some of the other Mario games out there, this one was released in 2012 and it brings Mario on a chase to find Princess Peach once again. He has to collect the coins that are all scattered across Mushroom Kingdom. The Koopalings are in full force within this game, so keep an eye out for them.

Another version of this game was later released, New Super Mario Bros. U. As one of the playable characters in Super Mario 3D World, he's just an average character. That's something that changes when it comes to the newest Super Mario Game, Odyssey.

SUPER MARIO 3D WORLD

Released in 2013, the gang ends up finding a fairy creature, known as a Sprixie. Bowser comes around, captures the creature himself and now the group has to go hunt down Bowser and save the Sprixie that he has taken. They enter into a whole new world, which opens up many different options for the players. The new world is known as Sprixie Kingdom.

They have to find out what Bowser wants with the Sprixies and what makes them so special to where he took them. The graphics of this game have improved compared to the last few games, making it well worth the time you spend checking it out. One of the best games of the year, Super Mario 3D World was highly praised by Mario fans, critics and standard Nintendo players alike.

Keep in mind, over the years, there have been many, many different Mario games released. With everything from the Olympics to racing to anything and everything in between, there have been countless gaming options with the little Italian plumber. The sports ones mostly did well on the gaming charts, and so did the racing ones on the Wii. If your favorite Mario-themed game isn't covered here it's still out there!

Play the Mario games you know and love and we encourage you to check them all out. Over time you just might build a unique collection of your own, that you want to come back to again and again.

Learn a bit more about Super Mario Odyssey and what you can expect from this game that's making every Mario fan excited with the possibility of something new and unique from Mario and his gang. Mario is able to do so much more in this game than you could ever imagine.

Check it out for yourself...

SUPER MARIO ODYSSEY STRATEGY

Mario never thought he would stray so far from home, but in an epic battle with Bowser for Princess Peach, he gets knocked out of the sky down to the Cap Kingdom in Bonneton. It's here that Mario befriends a bunch of new characters and he starts on a whole new epic mission. It's his job to stop Bowser and he won't have to do it alone.

The locals here are not only friendly, but they want to make sure that Bowser is stopped too! They are all ready to give Mario a hand at defeating him once and for all. Cappy, a friendly flying top hat wakes Mario to get him moving and to start working toward escaping Bowser's clutches once and for all.

So where does the Odyssey come from?
The incredible airship that Mario finds himself in command of is the Odyssey. He's able to travel between all of the kingdoms that are spread out throughout the world in search of

Bowser. He will go to each of the lands in search of this villain, only to find himself fighting through level after level before accomplishing his goal. It's not an easy fight, but one that Mario is prepared to take on!

This all-in-one strategy guide will help you get where you need to go to locate Bowser and stop him from marrying Princess Peach. While you'll be working toward stopping Bowser throughout this game, it's all the places and experiences that you see along the way that will really hold your attention.

Put on your top hat and prepare for a bumpy ride because the Odyssey is taking on the biggest (and best) adventure it has ever known, are you ready for the ride to come?

It is up to Mario — and YOU! to save the day and make sure Princess Peach is rescued in a timely manner... are you up for the challenge?

IMPORTANT THINGS, PLACES AND PEOPLE YOU'LL SEE

There are several items that you want to keep an eye out for while playing. Many of these things are going to come and go with each kingdom that you come across. Learn more about each of them and enjoy help getting through each kingdom, some additional points and a better shot at reaching Princess Peach.

HEARTS

These are an important icon to watch out for. Mario's max health is indicated by the three hearts on the screen. Taking a hit will remove one heart and losing all three hearts results in a K.O. It will cost the player ten coins, but Mario will reappear at the closest check point if this does happen.

Picking up regular hearts can keep Mario's heart gauge topped up and help you avoid losing coins and time while working through the level. These are found by breaking blocks or pounding the ground in specific areas.

There are also special hearts in the game known as power-up hearts. These have a gold ring around them and are wearing a crown. This is a power-up that can make Mario's health bar go from three hearts to six! However, if you get knocked down to three or less, the power-up

ends and Mario is back to his standard three hearts. These hearts are rare to find throughout the game, but they can also be purchased in Crazy Cap's shop or found when scanning Princess Peach's bridal amiibo. They're good to stock up on right before a particularly difficult level, so plan ahead!

THE COINS

Gold coins are what Mario is going to have the most contact with as he goes through the game. They can be picked up and held onto. You can find them in busted blocks, in the ground and even by defeating the wildlife in the areas. By cracking the ground, Mario is then surrounded by a ring of coins that he can pick up.

When you see the gold coins, they can easily be picked up just by walking over top of them. Just keep in mind that if Mario is K.O.ed then he has to pay for his life back with ten coins. Collect as many as you can for this purpose, but also to spend in Crazy Cap's Shop and Hint Toad's Power Moon clues that he often has available if you have the right amount of gold coins to spend on the hints.

Single coins go right in your pocket, while coin blocks hold up to 10 coins, coin rings are three coins, Regional coins are two, Power Moon coins are five, picking up hearts while having full health brings five coins, and finally there are coin piles that offer sometimes very large amounts, but they offer different amounts depending on the pile.

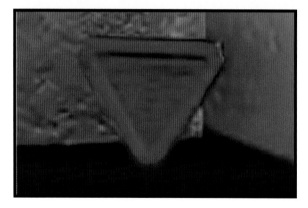

REGIONAL COINS

Regional coins are purple coins that are hidden throughout most kingdoms. They are the local currency and are somewhat rare to find. Usually the smaller kingdoms will give 50 coins throughout, while larger kingdoms give out 100.

These coins are useful as you can spend them within Crazy Cap's Shop when you'd like a unique item that can only be purchased through the use of the local currency for that kingdom. Hold onto all of the purple regional coins, as they're useful for specific purchases and for other purposes as well.

When the coins are collected, an outline will appear. Send either Cappy or Mario through the outline and you can collect two more gold coins.

CRAZY CAP'S SHOP

Crazy Cap's Shop presents Mario with a wealth of items that can be purchased and used throughout the game. Both purple and gold coins are able to be spent inside the shop. Gold coins can be spent at any of these shops, while purple coins have to be spent in the kingdom that they were found. Each is shaped differently depending on the kingdom that they are picked up in.

You can only purchase some items within Crazy Cap's Shop with purple coins, so it is important to take note of how many you have as compared to how many certain items cost. By taking the time to locate all the local currency offered throughout a kingdom, you can afford to purchase all of the unique items the shop has in stock.

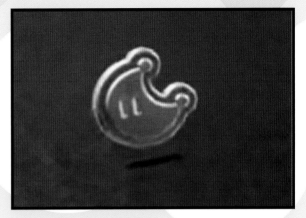

POWER MOONS

Mario's main goal is to find Bowser and to smack the stuffing out of him, but before he can do that and rescue his girlfriend he needs to gather enough Power Moons. Without those Power Moons travel isn't possible, so read on to learn exactly how you can track down the moons and get where you need to go.

MOON SHARDS

Sometimes the Power Moons are broken up into moon shards. There are usually five smaller chunks that have to be found to be put together to make one. You have to gather all five of the shards to create one whole Power Moon. There is an indicator that shows how many shards you have and how many more you need. Once all five are collected, the whole Power Moon will be shown nearby for Mario to collect.

Picking up Power Moons can refill Mario's heart bar, while picking them up underwater can refill oxygen. This is extremely valuable to remember, because it allows you to continue hunting for strings of moons more easily. Additionally, once you grab the Power Moon, you still can go back to the area later on and go through the Moon's outline. This grants five coins and can also refill your hearts or oxygen again, so learning their locations will help you even after you have the moon.

When you visit each new kingdom for the first time, you're going to need to find Power Moons to replenish and repair the Odyssey airship. Different kingdoms require different numbers of Power Moons, so pay attention to how many you need so you know when you're able to move on. The number of Power Moons that are needed are shown in dotted outlines that will fill as you collect them. Additional to these Power Moons, you also have to complete a local quest before you're able to move to the next kingdom.

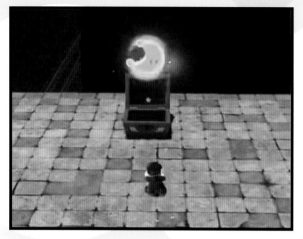

BURIED TREASURE

It wouldn't be a fun game without a little treasure hunt, would it?

Sure you'll find coins, Power Moons and hearts about in plain sight, but there's plenty of additional treasure buried down under the earth. Talkatoo provides pretty good hints for finding these hidden treasures in the ground, so listen closely.

Here are some other signs that there is hidden treasure nearby:

· Marks or cracks in the ground

· Glowing ground pieces

· Rumble from the controller when you're standing on a particular spot

· Mario sometimes gazes off to the spot where something is hidden

· Mario will toe the turf below him when something is amiss

OTHER ITEMS OF NOTE

There are many other items that you want to be aware of when moving through each of the unique kingdoms. Each item awards the user with plenty of points, coins and other goodies, so take note so you know when you're looking at something important.

CAT MARIO AND PEACH

These are old time pictures that are painted on some of the rock walls and other surfaces. When you find them, hitting Cat Mario with Cappy can award you with 10 coins, while hitting Cat Peach awards a heart.

BLOCKS

It just isn't a Mario game without blocks added to it. You're going to encounter a bunch of different blocks, so it's important to know what each one of them will reward you with.

DID YOU KNOW?

Some of the blocks you cannot even see! They're invisible until something hits them. If you find something amiss around the sky area, then give a simple jump up and see if there is a block that has been hiding there all along.

Brick blocks are the norm for Mario games and they will be busted apart when Mario hits them, revealing coins or other tokens. Steel blocks can be used to hang on, jump on or jump from but they usually do not give anything, but are there to be used as a platform.

? blocks are those blocks that give off a decent amount of goodies. Once hit though, they turn into steel blocks that are no good anymore. They give out coins, hearts, Power Ups, Power Moons and much more. You never know what you're going to get until you hit them and see what they have to provide you with.

Keep in mind, some brick and ? blocks might not go to steel blocks right away. Keep hitting the blocks for additional coins and prizes. Once they become steel, then they have nothing more to give.

PIPES

Just like in the original Mario games before, pipes are found throughout many of the lands. By going into them, you can be transported to new places and see new people along the way. Just jump or walk in them and see where it takes you. Some of these hidden places bring you to places that award more coins, hearts or Power Moons.

CHECKPOINTS

Just like in the original Mario game, checkpoint flags are located throughout the kingdoms. With Bowser's flag on them initially, Mario can pull that down and put his own on it. They can be found by using the map or going through the entire kingdom.

ROCKET FLOWERS

Throw Cappy at any of the rocket flowers in the game and have him throw them back. This turns into a nice rocket boost for Mario and he can run with the speed of light. Keep throwing the flowers at Cappy to keep the power up going.

P-SWITCHES

These provide the user with many different types of hidden effects. You might get blocks that you have to break for prizes, hidden vines that you can climb up for prizes or an assortment of other goodies that are waiting for you on the other side.

SCARECROWS

When you see scarecrows somewhere, they usually mean there is a timed challenge that is waiting for Mario. These platforms only appear when the challenge is activated. Place Cappy on the scarecrow during the challenge. Mario has to complete all of the tasks on his own while Cappy is sitting on the scarecrow's head.

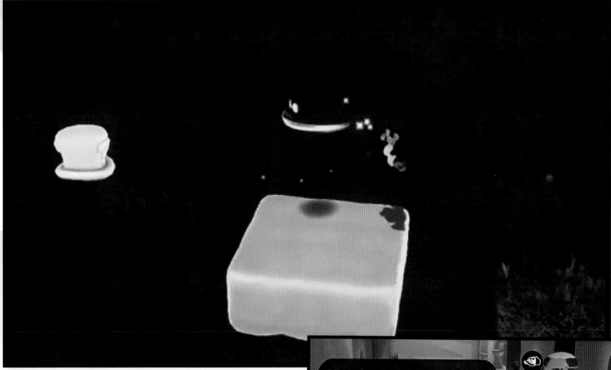

Mustache man, you're back!

HAT TRAMPOLINE AND LAUNCHER

The hat trampoline opens up when Cappy is thrown onto it, allowing Mario to propel himself higher or further. However, the launcher allows Cappy to be thrown a far distance, collecting coins and hearts as he goes. The launcher looks like two wheels on a triangle, while the trampoline looks like a flower that is closed until Cappy is thrown at it and then it opens.

PULSE BEAMS

Pulse Beams can be dangerous and you can be sure that if they're lit up, something around has activated them. These blocks are never just sitting around, and you need to be careful when in the presence of them. There are usually a handful in one place at any given moment. The expanding waves from these beams must be avoided, as they can take out bricks, blocks, wildlife and anything that stands in their way. They're tricky to jump over so be cautious when moving about an area when you see the beams.

KINGDOM LOCALS

Each area has its own set of locals, all different from the next. Speaking with them and learning more about the area is key to finding the Power Moons that are hidden within each of the kingdoms. Crazy Cap's Shop is usually located where all of the locals are, as well as locals that are in need of Mario's help. Complete the quests and become the hero.

TALKATOO

This feathered bird is a delight when you seek answers. He's found in each of the kingdoms perched atop a tree. He gives Power Moon clues by their names, allowing Mario to find some of them with ease. He can give up to three names of Power Moons at a time, which means you can go back and ask him for further clues on others once the first three have been found.

HINT TOAD

Another creature within the kingdoms that gives tips and tricks, this toad usually hangs out near Uncle Amiibo. He gives Power Moon finding hints to make the adventure a bit easier. However, his tips do not come without a price. You will have to pay Toad 50 coins for hints finding some of the most hidden Power Moons throughout the kingdoms.

Uncle amiibo

If you happen to have some, put 'em to work! They're good at finding any stray ⬤ Power Moons. Ⓐ

UNCLE AMIIBO

When Hint Toad begins scouting, he brings along Uncle Amiibo. He uses his special power to help locate Power Moons that are hidden in each kingdom. You can actually use this amiibo to get a free Hint Toad tip! However, this function can only be used every few minutes, so you will have to wait a bit before getting another hint.

CAP KINGDOM

BONNETON

You start the game in Cap Kingdom, where Mario lands after being pushed into the sky by Bowser. There are plenty of features and locations to take note of while in this cheerful place where many new friends can be found.

GETTING THROUGH CAP KINGDOM

Mario has to go through a series of steps to move onto the next kingdom. Here are some of the challenges he is going to come up against in his journey.

Team up with Cappy, whose sister Tiara was stolen along with Princess Peach by Bowser. Together, you will both go through the kingdoms and beat the quests that you come into contact with.

TO THE TOP OF TOP-HAT TOWER

All of the airships throughout Bonneton were destroyed by Bowser, so now Mario and Cappy have to come up with a way to make it across all of the kingdoms and get to where Bowser is. Cappy knows where there is an old airship and he thinks they can get it running.

Throwing Cappy against the wooden posts and towards enemies helps Mario collect coins along the way. It's an important skill to master, so make sure you're tossing Cappy around often. Toss Cappy at enemies and other wild creatures alike and you can take control of them, as well. Once in your power, you can use their special abilities (the frog provides high jumping capabilities) to make it through the rest of the level.

DEFEATING THE BOSS TOPPER

In order to get to the aircraft, Cappy and Mario have to defeat the boss that is waiting for them at the top of the tower. Topper is his name and he is quite angry that you have come to take the last aircraft. Topper will attack by using the three top hats that he is wearing. Once the attack starts, use Cappy to knock down the top hats from his head one by one so that he is unable to fight effectively. Mario can then leap up on his head. Once all of the top hats are knocked off, you have to go through the process all over again to win.

A Spark Pylon will appear once Topper has been beaten. Toss Cappy to capture it and then zip along the wire to the next kingdom.

- There are four regional coins high on a wall in the Frog Pond location. There are three more in Top-Hat Tower and three more in the poison peril area.

- Cap Kingdom also has 31 Power Moons hidden throughout, some of them can only be obtained after defeating Bowser. Hint: Bonneter Blockade, the Frog Pond and the Poison Tide.

SAND KINGDOM

TOSTARENA

Once you've gone through Cascade Kingdom, it is time to travel forward and take on the next challenge in Mario's quest. That challenge can be found in the town of Tostarena. It's a colorful, welcoming town with new friendly faces, new monsters to battle and of course more new Power Moons and coins to gather!

JAXI RIDES

Unlike Taxi rides that we all know so well, the inhabitants of this kingdom rely on Jaxi rides to get them where they need to go. Explore the desert in comfort and style when you take one of them out for a stroll.

COMPLETING THE QUESTS IN SAND KINGDOM

Of course, Mario needs Power Moons from the Sand Kingdom as well, and he's going to have to work hard to get them. Mario must move through the kingdom in search of Moons, as well as coins, hearts and other hidden treasures. With an itinerary set, make sure to go through each of the following steps for success in the Sand Kingdom.

THE HIGHEST TOWER

Once again it's up to Mario to journey to the highest point of the Kingdom to get farther in the quest line. You'll be tasked with locating and scaling the tallest tower in the region, so prepare for some tough work. On the way you'll also notice that Bowser's giant footprints are in the sand along the route you need to travel. You're getting closer!

Getting through the wall is just the beginning through. Once you break through that wall, you're going to have to walk through the Ancient Wall and go through paths and warp pipes to finally make it to the boss level. You'll have an opportunity to find a hidden Power Moon while venturing through the tunnels here, so keep your eyes open.

MADAME BROODE

At the end of the level, you're going to come across the boss's lair. Here you'll have to take on Madame Broode. She will prove a real challenge, but you have what it takes to overcome this tough boss, don't you?

While battling Madame Broode, pay close attention to the golden chain chompkins on a leash. This massive pet will determine whether you are successful or you fail. Follow the golden arrows on the ground and dodge out of the way when the chompkins come towards you. Throw Cappy at the pet to knock its hat off and then again to capture it. Once captured, you can put the chompkins to work fighting Madame Broode for you and that's when you'll make real progress.

Defeat her pet three times and you win and also get another Power Moon for your aircraft.

During a boss battle, check into the rocks. Break them open and Mario can usually find hearts hidden within, if he needs the extra help.

- 50 regional coins are located throughout this kingdom. You can find some of them atop a cliff, behind a red door and on the ledge of the 8-bit level.
- There are 40 Power Moons located throughout the kingdom, one you have to beat the boss for, some of the others are hidden in fossilized rocks, in a dinosaur nest, and in the secret path to fossil falls.

SAND KINGDOM

TOSTARENA

Once you've gone through Cascade Kingdom, it is time to travel forward and take on the next challenge in Mario's quest. That challenge can be found in the town of Tostarena. It's a colorful, welcoming town with new friendly faces, new monsters to battle and of course more new Power Moons and coins to gather!

JAXI RIDES

Unlike Taxi rides that we all know so well, the inhabitants of this kingdom rely on Jaxi rides to get them where they need to go. Explore the desert in comfort and style when you take one of them out for a stroll.

COMPLETING THE QUESTS IN SAND KINGDOM

Of course, Mario needs Power Moons from the Sand Kingdom as well, and he's going to have to work hard to get them. Mario must move through the kingdom in search of Moons, as well as coins, hearts and other hidden treasures. With an itinerary set, make sure to go through each of the following steps for success in the Sand Kingdom.

THE HIGHEST TOWER

Once again it's up to Mario to journey to the highest point of the Kingdom to get farther in the quest line. You'll be tasked with locating and scaling the tallest tower in the region, so prepare for some tough work. On the way you'll also notice that Bowser's giant footprints are in the sand along the route you need to travel. You're getting closer!

Go to the Tostarena Ruins Entrance and make your way up the stairs to the top. Note: To have Cappy come back sooner while moving around, just shake the controller and he will fly right back, so you can throw him again as you journey onward and upward.

While moving through this level you'll encounter tough Bullet Bill characters. To deal with them, you just have to capture them. This is the safest way to ensure that you can make it through the level. Fly the Bullet Bill through the rings, release them and then leap onto the platforms ahead.

Don't worry so much about searching for Power Moons while going through this level, you just need to focus on beating the level first because it's difficult. Dodge, dunk and use the flower launcher to make it through the twisting and turning hallways you have to follow through. Look for three crates towards the end of the level. Each will have something different inside of them: binoculars, a Power Moon and then a surprise.

You need patience and speed for this level, you'll have to move quickly and know when to dodge for success. Keep practicing and you'll get it with time.

BOTTOMLESS CANYONS

In this level you'll find a world underneath a world. With mountains of sand under the kingdom, you will go here to find Moon shards, but also regional coins that are left about. You may have to do some digging, but each of them can be found hidden below the levels of the kingdom above. You'll have to fight to get onto the platform that will bring you down, but throwing Cappy helps you get there easier.

You get a freebie right next to the Moe-Eye when you first enter, but from there, you have to search for the other shards. You can collect Moe-Eyes to use during this hunt, as well because their special sunglasses help them see things that are otherwise invisible to the naked eye.

INVERTED PYRAMID SHOWDOWN

If you're looking for a good fight in this level, you're in for a treat! Roll across the desert and enter into the inverted pyramid to see what is waiting for you there. You'll have to go through the 8-bit level in order to come out at the end for the final boss to defeat.

Keep an eye out for a large crack in the wall while working your way through the pyramid. This is where one of the Power Moons is hidden and you can easily break the wall to collect your prize.

Hariet is the boss of this level and she's not to be taken lightly. Between her hat and her ponytail she has a variety of special moves to use on you. She uses her hat to attack and her ponytail to throw bombs at you. If you can stay on one side of the arena and dodge the bombs, or use Cappy to knock them back towards her, then you can keep yourself alive while working on a strategy to take her out. If the bombs hit you or the floor in front of you, this can mean K.O.

She will continue to come at you with her hat and bombs, so step lightly and move around as needed throughout the fight. As time moves forward, Hariet will zig zag in front of you to make it harder and harder to get ahead

of her. All you have to do is jump on top of her head and she will be defeated. Do that and you'll be awarded with another sweet, sweet Power Moon.

THE HOLE LEFT BEHIND

Once you beat the boss, you'll be amazed by what the pyramid does. It actually lifts up and takes off leaving behind a massive hole in the ground Mario has to go into in order to finish his quest. However, before heading down into the deep dark abyss, make sure that you have all the Power Moons as well as any goods from the store you think you'll need. You don't know what awaits you inside.

The hole actually leads to an icy wonderland where you will meet yet another boss, once you make your way through the maze that they laid out for you. You have to use Cappy on the launcher in order to break the ice blocks overhead to make it through the maze.

Capture a Goomba to give you more traction while walking on the ice. They can sometimes slip, but it is less likely if you have one in your control.

If you continue through the maze, you will come across a Power Moon laid out for you as well as regional coins just behind it. The Binding Ring

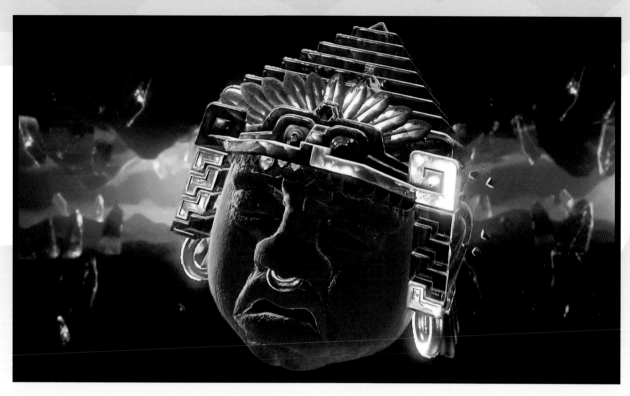

was once placed in this area, but it's currently out of place because Bowser took it. There is just a a bleak shadow left behind.

To get to the next boss at this point, capture a Bullet Bill and ride it across the gap.

KNUCKLOTEC

The boss that comes and meets you at the end of this icy level is Knucklotec. When he enters the room, he slams the floor and sends icicles raining down to the ground, some of them smashing open holding hearts. Notice where these are before the fight.

During the fight Mario will encounter flying fists. Watching for the shadows can help you dodge each one as it is sent next to you. It's important to also watch out for the falling icicles each time he smashes down on the ground because they're deadly and will quickly take you out of the fight if you aren't careful.

Dodge the fists and the icicles a few times and then you'll have your moment to strike! Knucklotec will grab you with his hands, it's now that you need to break free and then capture one of his hands to use against himself.Use Cappy to do this and once you do, he will be defeated. He also leaves behind a Power Moon.

If you defeat the boss but you're still stuck in the kingdom, you'll have to go back through the levels to search for all the other Power Moons that you left behind.

· There are 100 regional coins throughout Sand Kingdom. Some of them can be found along the way to meet the bosses.

· Look for 89 Power Moons all hidden or held throughout the kingdom. Check the ruins, leaning pillars, luggage, fountains and dunes to find some of them.

LAKE KINGDOM

LAKE LAMODE

Choosing Lake Kingdom connects the paths that Mario needs to follow in order to get to Princess Peach. In this area you'll discover plenty of mysteries and wonders, as well as meet new people along the way.

THE JOURNEY IN LAKE KINGDOM

Mario must go through a series of steps here in order to make it to the end. While working through this kingdom, just like all the others your priority should be on tracking down the Power Moons and on beating the bosses that will challenge you along the way.

Upon landing, the stairs are broken going into the Water Plaza, so Mario has to find another way in. It is possible to triple jump from the beach, toss Cappy to the top of the wall and then tackle jump up the landing. However, it can be a difficult move to master.

Cross over the water near where the ship landed. Bounce off the trampoline and bounce over the gates. Grab the coins that pop up and then grab the zipper and tug. This creates an opening for Mario to go through.

Make sure to stay lined up with the air bubbles ahead, collect the regional coins as you make your way through the path then take a right at the first fork that you come across. Collect the Power Moon from the treasure chest and you're in!

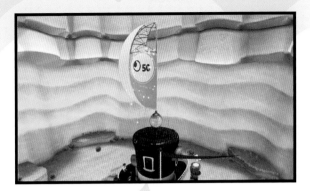

Make sure that you keep in mind that while Mario can swim under water he only has a limited supply of air! The meter on the side tells you when he is running out of air, so keep your eye on it and prepare to grab bubbles as needed. If anything, capturing a Cheep Cheep can give Mario a Power Up to breathe even longer while under water.

Swim through the rest of the maze under water and collect the Power Moons as you go. Make sure to stop and collect standard and regional coins along the way. You may have to break through some of the entrances in order to keep going. There are also five shards hidden along the way, so keep an eye out for those as you swim along.

One of the Power Moons that you will come to notice is on the back of Dorrie. Dorrie is extremely peaceful and she will let you take the Moon right off her back without a problem, so be nice to her.

WATER PLAZA LOWER LEVEL

The lower level of the Water Plaza welcomes you a sprawl of coins to gather up, you'll be raring to head to the item shop after a trip through here! Travel through the watery hallway to the left to go to the middle level of the plaza. There is a P-Switch there that you can hit to open the doorway and allow yourself entry into the room. Once there, you can lower down the trampolines, making it much easier to jump and reach the crates along the top. This is where another Power Moon is hidden.

Follow along with all of the following steps to make it through the kingdom and onto the next.

RANGO THE BOSS

Rango is a vicious boss equipped with a buzzsaw hat atop his head. He'll cut you apart with this aggressive hat if you aren't careful. During the fight make sure to stay out of range of the hat, and pay close attention to learn how Rango moves around. When he goes to throw his hat, throw Cappy at it and then bounce on the underside of the hat, which turns into a trampoline. Bounce on top of Rango's head and collect the Power Moon he drops after you bop him three times.

- 50 Regional coins are hidden throughout the kingdom, the red door has some behind it and the crack in the wall makes way for others.

- There are 42 Power Moons hidden throughout the kingdom, some of them are hidden and others are out in plain sight. Check the hidden passages, bodies of swimming water, secret zippers and cliffside to uncover each and every one of the hidden moons.

WOODED KINGDOM

STEAM GARDENS

Steam Gardens is a factory location within the Wooded Kingdom and it's the site for most of the Power Moons as well. Keep your eyes open and look around for all the hidden objects that you have to find while going through this level.

TAKING ON THE PATH AHEAD IN THE WOODED KINGDOM

Mario starts off his journey in the Wooded Kingdom at the southern reaches of the region. From there he has to move through all the challenges ahead, gather up the Power Moons and get all the power necessary to get the ship moving once again. It will prove a more difficult task than expected though, so buckle up and prepare for a serious fight!

Collect the regional coins that are atop the outer wall of the kingdom. Make sure to look up, as they're always hiding in this area.

THE DIRT PATH LEADS YOU ON

After making it through the Southern Reaches, follow along with the dirt path and buy as many Power Moons as possible from the Cap Shop along the way. Use the dirt path to travel to the Sphinx. Once you encounter the Sphinx it's up to you to give him the correct answer. Bowser wants flowers — once you do that you can move on to the Iron Road.

Orange and yellow blocks on the pathway will collapse under Mario's weight, so make sure to step lively now!

While walking down the Iron Road, stay on the path and avoid waking the angry T-Rex that's napping away peacefully on the road. Your quest is to take the seeds from the gardener and plant them in the pots that are found at the end of the path.

Toss Cappy at the purple poison, as well as the plant that spits it out to reduce your chances of getting hit with this stuff. It could come with bad results if you do! As long as you make careful use of Cappy along this road you should have no trouble moving on without getting poisoned and planting the seeds along the way. Make sure to use the ledges and other items to hop over the unsteady boards and get to the destination quickly.

This is one of the most complex levels that Mario is going to go through, so it is important to activate the Warp Flags each time you notice one. The flags are important markers that will help you avoid getting lost and keep you in the correct world the entire time.

FIGHT THE BIG POISON PIRANHA PLANT

In this fight it's up to you to best the massive man-eating plant. To do this toss Cappy at the rocks along the sides of the ledges to knock them down. You'll knock down a bunch that you can throw at the plant monster to stun it. Once you do that get as close as you can by throwing more rocks through Cappy and then jumping up on top of the plant head. Do this successfully a few times and you'll beat the plant and get rewarded with a Power Moon.

THE FLOWER THIEVES ABOUND

The next takes you through a glass chamber that shatters, making way to a P-Switch. Before you jump on it, find the gap in the ground and jump down there. While you're down there capture an Uproot, this will help you climb across the wall effectively. Go around the corner and up over the ledge. If you go to the proper spot you'll locate another Power Moon.

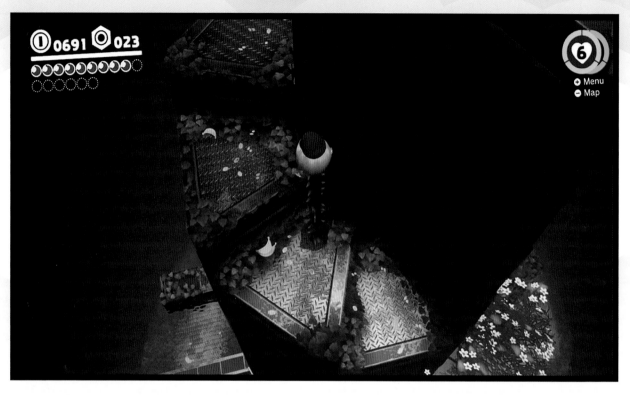

Step on the switch and a giant flower will bloom before you. Once it blooms follow along with the pathway that appears. Just make sure to go fast, as the flower does not last for long. Do the same thing when you get to the next flower.

Hit the P-Switch inside the tower and then follow the road you gain access to. Capture an Uproot to get a life heart that is hanging on the side of the wall. Stretch the Uproot's legs to reach the P-Switch above you. Crack open the nut that appears when walking through the path and you will find another Power Moon. Follow the path to the very top.

The flower road that you follow changes with time, and disappears and reappears at timed intervals. While climbing up the spiral staircase, make sure to jump on the shadow because there's another Power Moon up there.

SPEWART IS THE NEXT BOSS

When you walk outside on the top of the pathway, you will come face to face with Spewart. As his name suggests, this character spews poison out everywhere, leaving you with a very difficult fight. Make use of Cappy to clean up the poison each time he spews it out, then toss Cappy right at Spewart and jump up above him and ground pound him.

Once he is rolling around on the ground, throw Cappy at him again to knock his hat off. When his hat's off pound him one more time to finish him off. You'll easily defeat him with this strategy and he'll drop another valuable Power Moon. Now you're one step closer to making it through the Kingdom and getting to the princess.

THERE ARE VISITORS IN THE SECRET FLOWER FIELD

Earlier a flying object was spotted landing in the Secret Flower Field. Now it's up to Mario to go find out who these new visitors are. Take some time to go through the level up above to collect all the standard and regional coins, and the Power Moons, then go back down to the field to check out the new visitors that await.

Torkdrift is the one that has landed and he's looking for information about the area. To best this new boss you'll need help from an Uproot, so capture the creature before you get into the fight. Once you do, you can extend his legs and place pressure on the bulb that is coming from the aircraft. Crack it like you would with one of the nuts.

Mario has to do the same on the three cubes that appear, as these are what is giving Torkdrift his power. Crack each of them while on the move, to avoid getting hit with any of the lasers that Torkdrift shoots out during the battle.

Use the Uproot to break all the cubes, then head back to the dome to crack that. Once you complete this step you've bested Torkdrift and you'll be rewarded with yet another Power Moon.

· The Wooded Kingdom has 100 regional coins scattered throughout the region, some of them can be found in Sky Garden Tower or in the trunks of trees throughout the forest.

· There are 54 Power Moons placed throughout this Kingdom. Many of them are given after quests, but you can find them as you go along too. Some are invisible, so it is good to look around for shadows. Always check in rock cracks along the way to avoid missing moons!

CLOUD KINGDOM

NIMBUS ARENA

Along his travels Mario can't help but stop in the location where happiness comes to life, the Cloud Kingdom. Up here is where the Doves live, and they're home is known for tranquility and beauty, but there are going to be some real challenges for you here as well. Everyone that visits the Cloud Kingdom decides that they want to move there, and for good reason, it's irresistible!

COME FACE TO FACE WITH BOWSER

Congratulations! You've caught back up with Bowser in one of the most peaceful looking locations in all of the Mario Universe, but you have your most intense fight yet to deal with. It's time to take Bowser on hat-to-hat so get ready for a serious battle.

When Bowser jumps on the platform, he means business. He'll tosss his hat at you, and it's designed to deliver a series of punches when it gets close enough. Be smart and counter the hat with Cappy to keep it from doing damage. A proper throw with Cappy will knock Bowser's hat upside down, letting you claim it for yourself.

Put on the hat and know that some extra powers await you when you do. Once wearing the hat you'll be able to move through the rings of fire unharmed, and you need to run after him when he tries to get away. Once Bowser grows tired, use his own hat against him with as many hits as you can get in. Bowser's hat will knock him out and you've won the first battle! Unfortunately it's not the only one you'll face.

Once Bowser wakes back up he's tougher than ever before. He has two purple hats to attack with now and they can do serious damage if you aren't careful. The strategy is different this time though. You shouldn't throw Cappy at the purple hats, but at the white hat atop Bowser's head. Hit the white hat and the purples will be removed. Once you do this Bowser will run once again and you must chase him and attack just as before. This concludes round two!

- There are 9 Power Moons here, but you must come back to get them after you have gone through other kingdoms.

LOST KINGDOM

FORGOTTEN ISLE

This is a run down place that holds a lot of mysteries. It's up to you to uncover the mysteries of this ancient place on your own if you want to make it to the next kingdoms. Go through the area with care, and prepare for the challenges that await on your way to Princess Peach.

MARIO HAS A QUEST TO TAKE ON!

Mario faces some serious challenges in the Lost Kingdom so prepare to work hard and overcome each one that comes your way. It won't always be easy, but it's worth the effort I promise!

RESCUE CAPPY!

Klepto has come around and swooped up Cappy! It's up to you to get him back. The snatch happens when you're headed north towards the bridge. Klepto swoops down and snags Cappy right off your head and heads towards Swamp Hill! You'll have to travel there and get him back, but take care, because the going is much tougher without Cappy to aid you.

Advance to the ruins that have the strange starburst shapes on them. Go to the side and pound on one of the starburst. One side will raise, while the other falls and then pounding again creates a teeter-totter effect. Keep climbing up and using the starburst as you go. Travel up to the top of the stairs — this is where Cappy is being held.

Patiently wait for the wigglers to make their way past, and be careful not to engage them, without Cappy they'll prove very difficult enemies. Once you do, run up the stairs and make Klepto follow you back down. Once he is on one side of the ruins, hit the starburst which will fling Klepto up into the air — making him drop Cappy so you can grab him and keep going.

COLLECT ALL THE POWER MOONS YOU NEED

Now that you have Cappy back – congratulations about that by the way! – it's time to start on your next mission. It's one that involves Power Moons, so prepare for a bit of treasure hunting. You'll have to journey around the kingdom and seek out each and every one of those Power Moons until you have enough to continue traveling. This takes some time so be patient.

Of course, keep a close eye out for Klepto during your search, as he likes picking up treasure and grabbing them up whenever he can and might take Cappy again!

TIPS

- This level has 35 Power Moons hidden throughout. Make sure that you check below the cliff's edge, in the caves, in the rock ledges and even in with the butterflies you find along the way.

- The region also has 50 regional coins to find. Some of them are hidden by the Power Moons and others are found in other areas. Make sure you look up high everywhere you go!

METRO KINGDOM

NEW DONK CITY

This city looks just like a city when you land there, so don't be surprised at the sight of some serious sky scrapers. There is a lot to see and do and Mario will have his hands full trying to get through this level with all the quests and Power Moons that he needs to collect.

MARIO TAKES ON THE CITY AHEAD

Mario needs 20 Power Moons to make it to the next level. To get most of them he's going to have to complete challenging quests. Get started lending a helping hand to the people of the city and the moons will start rolling in.

The Mayor of the city needs help restoring the power back to the city. Even though Bowser has already been there and talked about his wedding, now it is time for the mayor to think about the citizens that are living there. Can Mario help her out?

Ride down the spark pylon to the outskirts of the city. Make sure to swat all the larvae that you come into contact with using Cappy before they hatch, or they might cause further problems later on. Be careful to sidestep the larvae and try not to get in their way, they have amazing tempers and they literally blow up when someone stands before them.

Better yet, grab a scooter and you can run right over those larvae as you pass them. Plus, you can get around the outskirts a bit easier and with more style when you're on one of the scooters.

Since one of Bowser's advertisements is in the pathway you need to travel down, you'll have to take the other path and drive past the Sherms to the City Hall. Go into the construction site from there. Capture a Sherm to use on this level and drive to the nearest suspended beam. Here you'll want to travel up to the ? block and use Cappy to strike it.

Go through the construction site, where you'll locate another Power Moon. Then you can skirt around to the front of City Hall.

From here, you can capture one of the Sherms that's blocking the doorway and use it to blast the other Sherms out of the way. Just make sure to fire constantly, because you don't want them to catch you! Be careful to wipe out any larvae heading your way with the Sherm as well.

Now climb up to the first rooftop. Use a series of wall jumps or the spark pylon to get across to the heliport. Look above the swaying beam and grab the Power Moon that is resting there. Now enter into the City Hall from the door in the adjacent building to where you are.

Run across the crumbling areas, down to where the striped poles are. Jump down here, taking care to skip the next landing to go even further. Leap from pole to pole across from you to get to the treasure chest that's waiting on the other side.

Finally, use the Spark Pylon to get to the rooftop where you're going to meet the boss of this level, a mechanical beast with quite the temper.

Mechawiggler is the beast that so many are afraid of, but it's your duty as Mario to battle him. Use a Sherm to blast through this beast with all your might. He is going to be spitting and spewing at you, so blast him while moving around to dodge the attacks. You can't stop for anything or you'll take serious damage almost immediately. Use the Sherm to blast in the areas where it seems like he is folded into himself. This will eliminate more than just one section of his body, allowing you to win faster.

Once he goes dark, you can stop blasting but then he will turn gold after a bit. He's invincible now, but don't worry, you won't have to battle him any longer. He'll disappear through a portal and you'll be brought down to a platform where you can move on with your journey.

HELPING THE CITY GET A FRESH START

Since the destruction of the Mechawiggler, the city has changed including the Warp Flags and the rain that wouldn't stop before. Come morning, the city is back to itself and Bowser's ads are all removed from the city limits.

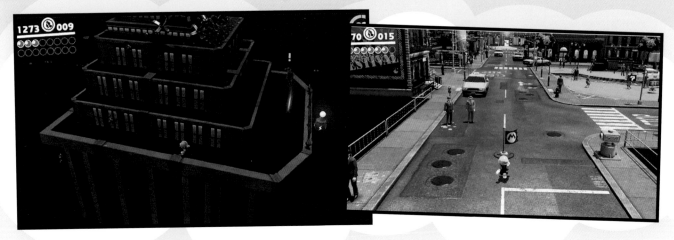

Go to City Hall to find Mayor Pauline and help her find four musicians that can play in the festival that she is putting together. The first one is right outside of the City Hall. He is a drummer. Once you talk with him, you're presented with a Power Moon. The next musician can be found in the Mayor Pauline Commemorative Park, he is a bassist. Use the Spark Pylon to get here as fast as possible.

Use the poles on the side of the building outside the Cafe to flick Mario up to the rooftop. Talk with the trumpeter that is waiting on the top of the room to get another Power Moon. The last musician can be found on Main Street in the corner of the park. He is a guitarist that is also going to provide a Power Moon.

TIME TO POWER UP THE STATION

In order to get the most from the festival, Mayor Pauline needs a bit more help from Mario. This time, he has to lift open the manhole and go into the sewers of the city. The manhole is located in front of the cafe.

This is the underground power plant. To get things started you'll want to go down the walkway and into the second pipe. Spin each of the platforms to help you get from one side to

the next. Do this by throwing Cappy to get the platform spinning, a bonus to this technique is that it also helps to keep the poison away from you. With the platforms in motion it's up to you to jump from one to the next to get around. At the top ledge of this platform, there is a Power Moon hidden right above it.

Mayor Pauline will meet you down by this platform before you can reach the Power Moon. It's here that you'll have to fight a poison plant. Defeat the poison plant to stop the poison from being sent everywhere and earn another Power Moon in the process. Now all you have to do is ground pound the red button on the floor to get the festival started!

PUTTING ON A TRUE FESTIVAL

The glorious festival has begun, and you're busy celebrating and having a good time, but of course there's another challenge for you to get through. During the big event you're taken up on stage with the band and a new mural is erected on the side of one of the buildings that looks just like Mario himself. This is for all your help with the city and how thankful they are.

You will have to go through an 8-bit level and it can take some time to master. Just keep your patience and go through the level as smoothly as you can. Avoid any of the barrels and fire pits that come into play, while also hitting the blocks for coins. This is from back in the classic Mario days, so it is a bit of an enjoyment level before moving onto the next kingdom.

Once you make it through the 8-bit level, you are awarded with another Power Moon. Just like the 80's classic. Enjoy this complex level, it adds another element of fun to the game and creates some challenges that you aren't likely to encounter during other areas of the game.

COLLECT MORE POWER MOONS

Now all Mario has to do is collect enough Power Moons to power up the aircraft and fly out of there. With so many of them hiding around this city, a little searching is all it takes to build up the collection high enough.

Check out each of the following locations when moving through the city. Rooftop flower pots, RC car racing grounds and in the park where you found the guitarist. You're not able to leave until you have collected enough to repair the Odyssey and to keep flying to the next levels.

- The area contains 100 regional coins that are hidden as you go along the various quests. while moving about you need to look up on the rooftops and balconies, as you drive the scooter. There are many nooks and crannies, but most of the regional coins for the area are out in the open.

- The area also contains a high number of Power Moons to collect, with 81 total in the area. You already know how to come across some of them, but make sure to hop on the buildings, in the trash and to question Captain Toad and to search in the cafe.

SNOW KINGDOM

SHIVERA

This is the land of ice and snow and it is where Cappy and Mario land next. It is a land where shivering is a common occurrence, but the locals are friendly and warm. The area is simple to get through and most of the quests are quite short, which is good for us because we're already getting chilly!

MARIO'S QUESTS FOR THIS ICY KINGDOM

Just like the previous kingdoms, Mario has quests he must fulfill to get the Power Moons to get the Odyssey up and running. In order to do this though, he's going to have to battle through each of the quests.

On top of the snowy plateau, you will find a mound of snow. Throw Cappy at it to knock off the snow and then dive down into the well below.

GOING THROUGH FOUR MAIN ROOMS

Bowser has taken off with a cake and now Mario has to chase after him in order to get it back. He is going to have to go through four different rooms along his journey. This was a great gift planned for the after-the-race festivities, so now Mario has to catch up to him to try and get it.

Wander through the halls once you land in the city below through the well. You will come across four different rooms with objectives in each one.

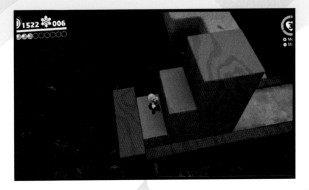

THE ICICLE CAVERN

This is a slippery area and it's easy to slide right off to your doom. That's why you need to make heavy use of Goombas while traveling here. They offer more traction, while also working to break down the icicles. If you notice a dangling shadow above you, use the Goomba to gently coax it down and make sure it does not fall on Mario!

When you have at least four Goombas you can open up a wall of ice and uncover Power Moons that are hidden behind it. Once you collect the two Moons here, you can bound up the stairs, being careful to dodge the icicles and slippery terrain. At the top, you will find even more Goombas that you can use along the way.

In the corner of the top room, you'll notice a stack of crystals in one of the corners. Use a Goomba to knock this stack apart and then break it to make way for the Power Moon to come out, but also for the exit pipe to show up.

HOLLOW CREVICE

Head to the top right spoke next. This is a room with square water pools filled up. There are five Power Moons hidden in this level and you have to run around and collect them all. Oh! There are also going to be BiteFrosts and of course, monsters that jump up at you

so battle your way through the room while making sure they don't get you. Try to stay out of the water, since there aren't any hidden shards to find in this area.

Jump to the top, collect the last Power Moon and use the pipe to get out of there once they have all been collected.

SNOWY MOUNTAIN

The left spoke is where the next little room is located. Use the hat trampolines to get in there and to the tops of the room to collect the coins and other goodies that have been left behind. There is a gap in the wall, throw Cappy to remove the snow that's build up here and then enter the crevice. Follow the hallway until you reach the end, where you will find another Power Moon. Go around the corner where you're going to find another boss to battle.

RANGO THE BOSS

Rango is an intense boss that makes use of blazed buzz saw hats to try and take you out. This villain is going to do anything possible to keep you from succeeding in your quest, allowing Bowser to escape once and for all. Break the rocks in the floor during the battle to unearth hearts, just make sure to keep your footing, as it can become quite slippery.

Block the hat throws that Rango makes with Cappy and by doing so you'll create a set of trampolines that you can use against Rango himself. All those flipped hats can be used to jump up on Rango's head. Hop up there and you'll do damage to the boss. Rango will go a little crazy after getting hit and then go back to throwing. You have to do the same moves and jump on his head again to finish him off. He will walk away after this and you will receive another Power Moon.

WIND CHILL CAVERN

This is a frosty place. Travel down through the bottom left spoke. The one serious danger present in Wind Chill Cavern is violet goo, so avoid it as much as possible. It can mean death if you land in it. Make it through this room and you'll start racing in the Icy Kingdom once again.

The entire room is moving and Mario must jump from Ty-Foo to Ty-Foo without losing his footing. The moment you lose your footing, you'll end up in the goo, which means death and we don't want that. You want to make sure that you keep in mind that these gusts will knock you down, so be quick but keep your footing.

Travel to the archway where the Power Moon is hidden and grab it before descending back down to the moving platforms. Take care of the Spinies on the lower platform and then reveal another hidden Power Moon.

BE PART OF THE RACE

To start up the race, head down the tube into the Snowline Circuit. There is a waiting room off to the right. Enter there and sit and wait for the next race to begin.

When you're ready to get in the race, you will be against seven others. Over the length of the course you'll be challenged by four wide 90 degree turns, so tread with caution. There are many tricks and traps that you'll encounter while going through the course so pay close attention and keep your eye on the road ahead. When you first try to get into the race the locals aren't willing to let him join because he's small and not well-suited to the environment, Cappy can help you be part of the action though.

Shiverian Elder

Our 🔔 Frost-Frosted Cake was stolen, so the prize will be

Since Cappy is able to capture the things in front of him, you just have to throw Cappy out to the driver and you can capture it to use in the race. You can use all their driving abilities, which helps maintain control of the car — this race is for the locals, after all.

You must be mindful of the traction as you round the corners. Keep a close eye on your opponents and make sure to give it some gas. To enhance your speed during the race, bound whenever you have a large amount of straight space ahead of you, just be careful to avoid bounding with a corner coming up because you can't turn until after. The winner gets a Power Moon at the end.

A Cheep Cheep can help you stay alive while you swim in the water for both warmth and oxygen. Capture one for longer periods of time in the icy waters.

- There are 50 regional coins to find hidden throughout the kingdom. Some of the places to check for them include bottomless looking pits, high up in the clouds and in the waiting room in Snowline Circuit where you waited to start the race.

- There are also 55 Power Moons to find as you go along. You get some for defeating the bosses that you come across, but you can also get them in random areas such as in the shining snow, at the entrance of the town, swimming in the freezing water and slipping behind the ice walls.

SEASIDE KINGDOM

BUBBLAINE

Welcome to the wonderful kingdom of Bubblaine, where anything is possible and where water rules the world around the inhabitants. Mario must go through this level in order to get closer to Princess Peach. It's up to you to make sure he completes the quests and gets the right amount of Power Moons to keep moving forward, so pay attention.

MARIO'S QUESTS FOR THE SEASIDE KINGDOM

Just like the other kingdoms before, Mario must complete quests and obtain the right amount of Power Moons in order to move onto the next level. You can expect a real challenge while working through this water Kingdom.

WHERE DID THE SPARKLE WATER GO?

Upon arrival, Mario will speak with a snail-like creature that calls this kingdom his home. He shows Mario the fountain used to fill up the area with bubbly-like sparkle water but currently, the glass is half empty and they need help finding out why and how to fix it. Mario realizes the pipes are clogged up, so he must go around to all four and unclog them.

STONE PILLAR

The stone pillar is the first seal that Mario has to unclog. The switch that will unclog this area is right offshore, but on a tall piece of land. Use a Gushen to propel Mario up to the top of the land so he can ground pound the switch and unclog the seal. Once this is completed, you'll receive a Power Moon for your efforts.

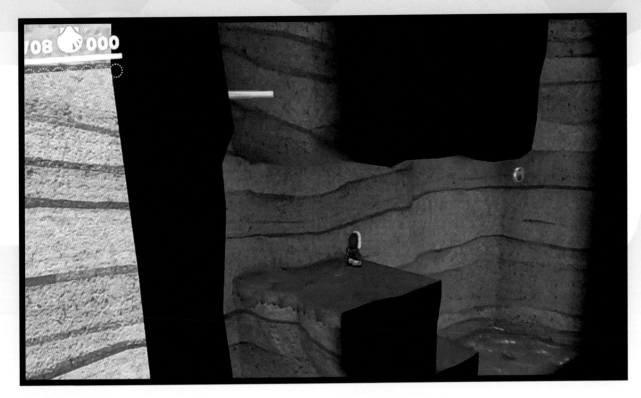

LIGHTHOUSE

The switch to unclog this seal is resting atop the lighthouse but you have to take an indirect route to get there. Go to the northern area of land and find a well. Once you locate the well, take a deep breath and jump in! This leads straight to the lighthouse.

At the bottom of the well you'll reach an underground tunnel underneath the lighthouse. Use a Cheep Cheep to get through this section. You'll need all the air you can get to make it through the hallways, be sure to keep an eye out for the Maw Rays lurking around corners and in cracks while exploring. These can actually kill Mario if they end up hitting him, so you will want to swim clean and fast through the tunnels as the Cheep Cheep.

Once the screen starts to shake, a giant Maw Ray will jump out and snap at Mario. Keep swimming and dodging the attacks that will come throughout the hallway. Be sure to collect all of the regional coins as you go. At the end, the screen will shake again, just keep to the middle of the screen, because many Maw Rays are going to attack. Just keep swimming.

Cross over the tunnel and then you have made it to the top of the lighthouse. You want to ground pound the switch and once this is activated you will receive another Power Moon.

HOT SPRING

On your way to Hot Spring Island make sure you check out Sand Bar Island. Look under the bar to find a hidden Moon that has been purposely placed there. You'll need to ground pound to unearth it. While here, go through the small tunnel holding your breath along the way. About halfway you will find a Power Moon, which restores your oxygen and health before reaching the end of the tunnel.

Once you get there, the hot springs are going to be covered in molten lava. Capture a Gushen and use it to spray water over the lava to cool it down, flying back and forth over it. Once you're up in the air, you can shake the controller to use a 360 water spin action to put out the lava.

After the lava is under control, hit the warp flag and then dive into the pool below. You will find a Power Moon hidden there, along with the next switch that works to unclog the seal.

ABOVE THE CANYON

The seal heading to the Sparkle Water Fountain is the last one that needs to be broken. Touch the warp pole at the bottom of the canyon, because this is a checkpoint. Capture a Goomba and then start your trek up the side of the canyon walls. Just make sure to watch for the angry Goombette that might be waiting there. If you rendezvous with the fairest Goomba there, you can collect another Power Moon.

Ditch the Goomba and run up the side of the canyon. Just make sure to jump over and dodge any shells that come tumbling down along the way. Once you get to the top of the canyon, there will be three boxes. You want to break them open using Cappy and then collect the Power Moon. Once you do this, the switch for the last seal will come out. Ground pound this to unclog the seal.

Now the octopus that thinks he's the master of the kingdom has been knocked off his perch and he's angry and seaking revenge!

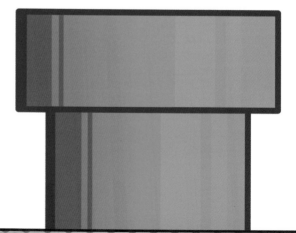

BRIGADIER MOLLOSQUE-LANCEUR III, DAUPHIN OF BUBBLAINE

When he arises, you will notice that he's covered in lava, your first task is to cool him down as much as you can. Capture another Gushen and use the spray feature to cover the octopus in water. Do your best to get him in the face. Start off spraying close to the octopus and then move away after you start your attack for the best possible shot.

As a Gushen, he will have a hard time chucking shells at Mario, so keeping away from him and flying over his head is a good idea. As long as you fight him properly, the Octopus boss is going to get furious, and the moment he does he will begin throwing drill bit pieces towards you. Dodge them while continuing to spray at him. Of course, you're going to want to ground pound him a few times.

Once you get his health most of the way down, set your aim to the top of his head and use a super ground pound to knock him out. You will have to continue to do this until he runs away, usually all it takes is around three times. You receive a Power Moon once he is defeated.

- 100 purple regional coins can be found throughout the region. Check in the high places, as well as the tunnels hidden throughout the lands under water.

- 71 Power Moons can be found throughout the kingdom, but Mario only needs 10 to keep flying. Some of the areas that these can be found include nesting spots, the back of the canyon, in the waves and in the glass palace treasure chest.

LUNCHEON KINGDOM

MOUNT VOLBONO

Everything is cooking hot with a volcano, so you can expect this kingdom to be none other than the hottest. Volcanic eruptions are happening all the time here, so keep a close eye on when and where they are occurring, so you're prepared for any eruptions that might come close to you. Anything can happen!

WHAT IS ON MARIO'S QUEST LIST

Luncheon Kingdom is jam packed with tough quests, but don't worried, your efforts won't go unnoticed! You'll be rewarded with not only great food and good times, but also Power Moons which you need to keep your journey

running smoothly. You can see Bowser's ship flying in circles overhead, which is just more motivation to keep moving because you're getting dangerously close to the villain once and for all.

REMOVING UNWANTED VISITORS

The townspeople are very nice and welcoming, but when someone visits that they do not want, they want to have him removed. It is up to Mario to find these unwanted guests and make sure that they leave the nice people alone.

Go to the Old Town to do some exploring. Capture a Goomba and then put all of the specimens in a stack. Head for the giant piece of corn and dodge all the dangers that are lurking in the way. This looks like a giant corn cob, bigger than little Mario and it should be towards the corner of the room.

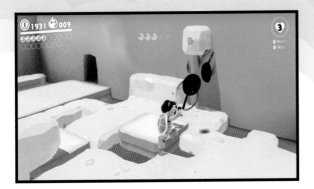

Jump up on the giant corn and walk towards the stack of Goombas that you've created. You can use this corn as a rolling platform while going over lava. Bring the captured Goomba stack to the Goombette by grabbing them and rolling over the lava with the corn. Once you do so, you're gifted with another Power Moon.

Go to the little pathway made of acid-water. Capture a Lava Bubble and swim through the pathway to get out at the other side.

BOSS SPEWART HAS BEEN AWAITING YOU

Spewart is known to spit out poison, so it is up to you to stay away from the spurting that he does. You don't want to be caught in it when it is being spit out and you don't want to step in it, so make sure to dodge and weave throughout this fight.

You will make Spewart mad, but use Cappy to knock the hat off his head. Without it, he is useless and will begin to jump around. After his hat has been knocked off, you have to move quick and bounce on top of his head. Once you do this, you'll be well on your way to winning the fight, but you'll have to repeat your steps a few times for real success.

Once you finally win the fight you get another Power Moon to add to your collection, so keep up the good work and the Odyssey will be flying around in no time!

THOSE CHEESE ROCKS LOOK TASTY, DON'T THEY?

Mario has to climb higher in the mountains, but he has to go down to the town for a bit. The giant stew pot that once held the delicious stew is now empty and much too hot to touch. Bowser has come and taken the food to claim as his own. Mario has to help the town get their stew back, while also saving the peppered meat that is now in peril.

Go through the narrow alleyway right by Crazy Cap's building and walk down it. You will come to a large pile of crates laying there. Break through the crates to get some goodies, including another Power Moon.

Notice the long pillars throughout the town. These are great for power jumping to and fro. There's a special technique you need to use to get to the top of the pillars though. Triple jump to get to the proper height for the pillars, and once you're up there you'll find a Power Moon just waiting for you to come and grab it.

Next, new ingredients must be found and then added to the pot to get the stew cooking. This next step helps the pizza owner throw in some delicious ingredients to get it going. Just make sure to not touch the pot — it is still too hot!

And the volcano is STILL erupting!

Look for three golden turnips hidden throughout Luncheon Kingdom. Add all three to the pot and each of them will give a Power Moon reward. One of the turnips is hiding right next to Crazy Cap's Shop. Throw a hat at the sprout to pick it out of the ground. Pick up the turnip and then take a running leap to throw it up and into the pot.

Next, go to the bubbling lava and capture Lava Bubbles to throw into the pot. They will become the delicious tomatoes for the stew. Be careful that you do not touch the side of the pot, as this is very hot! Once you throw one in, collect your Power Moon reward!

THE BIG POT WELCOMES YOU

As the townspeople continue to collect ingredients to add to the pot to make another stew, you have to be prepared to dive right in when they need you too.

Go past the Meat Plateau checkpoint and into the narrow path. You are going to pass a decent amount of Fire Bros and Magmatoes. Follow the path, go over the skinny bridge over the open air until you get to a wall that has a Volbonan stuck in it. Release this townsperson and go further up the wall to release another.

Continue to move up the wall and find not only a checkpoint, but also a giant piece of spiced meat that is ready for the pot! You'll need to crack through that hard salty shell in order to get the meat free. Before you jump off the wall though, you can look over and notice that there is a Power Moon to your side.

A giant bird is going to swoop down, so grab the Moon, grab the Meat and then jump down the wall. Remember, Mario doesn't take fall damage, so you do not have to worry about his health when you make it to the bottom of the ledge.

CASCADING MAGMA IS THE NEXT STEP

All of this ruckus has caused a commotion through the entire kingdom. Now there is a bird flying around the pot, the meat is free from the clutches of the salt and the pot is bubbling and boiling. A shift in the world has caused another piece of land to show itself. It's crowded by lava pathways.

You will have to explore this new land, but in order to do so, you have to wrap around the rock walls all the way around. You don't want to find yourself falling into any of the lava as you go, so keep a firm hold as you shimmy.

Go to the Volcano Cave Entrance flag, here you'll enter into the volcano. You will have to go up in the 8-bit playing field since there is such a wide gap between the entrance and where you stand.

Now all you have to do is roll the corn cob across the lava floors and jump to collect the regional coins in this area. Swerve to the left and right to collect more. Go up the pathway and then enter into the volcano's entrance.

The moment you walk in, you'll fall into the geysers. Once you do look to your side and you'll notice a sheer curtain covering a room to the side of you. This is where another Power Moon is hidden. Run into the room and grab it before continuing on.

Go into the alcove and use a Lava Bubble to swim over to where there are three lanterns. Use the bubble to light them up, revealing the next Power Moon that's hidden within the depths of this volcanic cave.

Going around this way allows for rear access to the mountain.

SHOWDOWN WITH A COCKATIEL

Next up is the showdown that you have been waiting for. This large bird boss has been following you all around the kingdom since you took that last piece of salted meat. Make sure

you enter into this section with care, using the walls around you to leap from, while making sure not to touch the plants that stick out from the sides.

While going down the pathway, use the side stones to avoid the rolling veggies, while also helping you get to the end of the pathway quicker. Trying to jump over them might be tricky, as they can be quite large.

Once you get to the end, you must keep going. The only way to go is through a Lava Bubble that you capture and then swim across to the next platform.

Cookatiel will meet you at the end of the platform and that's when the fight begins. Watch out for the spikes that he spits from his mouth and down into the stew. Always keep your eyes on him, since anything can happen when you drop your attention for any period of time. The bird will spew out liquid everywhere. This is poison, so avoid it at all costs.

All you have to do is watch where he is spewing, grab a Lava Bubble and jump on his head. Once you do this, you can keep jumping until he gives in and flies away.

- There are 100 regional coins throughout the kingdom. Make sure to check out all the high places, as well as those that go through the bubbling lava.

- 68 Power Moons are floating around the area. Some you have to earn, some you can purchase and some you can find hidden in certain places such as on top of taller mountains, in the cheese rocks and at Captain Toad.

RUINED KINGDOM

CRUMBLEDEN

You're one step closer to the real deal and actually going up against Bowser. With all of the kingdoms that you have left behind, it's no wonder you're running out of steam. Now it is time to challenge yourself a bit more then fly straight ahead, because what awaits you after this is going to be a lot of work. Are you ready to accept the challenge?

MARIO'S PLANS FOR THE AREA

Just like all the other Kingdoms, it's up to Mario to take on the quests, track down the regional coins and gather up all the Power Moons in this kingdom as well.

THE LORD OF LIGHTNING CALLS TO MARIO

You will have to battle the Lord of Lightning in order to get out of this kingdom and go onto the next.

Go to the swords in the ground and use Cappy to pull each of them up out of the earth below. Each of them is going to reveal coins, while the end one is going to give a Spark Pylon. Ride the pylon to wherever it leads — there is nowhere else to go, is there?

The Pylon brings you to the second tallest tower that you see off in the distance earlier on. While up here in this intimidating location you'll naturally run into one of Bowser's greatest weapons — the Ruined Dragon.

The dragon is puzzled at first when he notices Mario at the edge of his basin. Make sure to keep your distance, because he's not puzzled for very long and then he breathes out lightning. Dodge the lightning when you can, but the best way to stay out of the way is to keep your distance.

Once he goes through the shots and then the rings, you will notice he sends jolting waves of electricity through the ground. Mario must use his jump rope practice here and jump over the electricity as it comes to him. Once this ends however, Mario must be ready to jump on the dragon's face.

Use Cappy to remove the swords that are lodged in the top of the dragon's head. Once removed you can remove the cap that is controlling him. With the swords removed, the crown cracks and becomes vulnerable. This leaves Mario open for a ground pound.

Throughout this entire fight you'll be dodging the Burrbos that come popping up. You only have a limited time to remove the swords and then ground pound him. You need to be quick, so step lively and get the job done.

If you need life during this battle, check the outside ring of the arena for glowing spots. These are where you you'll find some hidden hearts to revitalize you as needed.

You'll must ground pound the dragon's head three times in order to defeat him. You will get a Power Moon with every pound that you make on his head, which is enough to get you the heck out of there!

- Ruined Kingdom does not hold any regional coins, so you don't have to keep an eye out for these while visiting this deserted kingdom.

- There are 10 Power Moons in total that can be collected here, but not all of them can be found upon the first visit. You must come back to collect the rest.

BOWSER'S KINGDOM

BOWSER'S CASTLE

By now, you've probably realized you're going to have to visit Bowser's castle in order to find Princess Peach. You should rejoice knowing that you made it this far in the Odyssey. With such a long journey, you'd think that it would stop here — but it doesn't. Make sure to collect more Power Moons and keep on moving along after the quests that await you here.

JOURNEY THROUGH... TO BOWSER YOU GO...

Go past the advance gate, check out the Goomba guards on patrol and make a stack with them by capturing them one by one. Head to the right, then follow the curl around the hallway. This leads to a special button. You must have a stack of 10 Goombas in order to get it to work. Luckily for you, you should already have them all gathered up at this point.

Hop onto the stack to get the Power Moon that's just above you on the ledge. Then grab the regional and gold coins waiting for you. Grab the Spark Pylon that shows up after you do this.

You will land in a floating courtyard. Make sure to grab the checkpoint here, in case something happens to you during the rest of your trip. Capture a Pokios and then flick yourself up to the roof to grab the Power Moon. Once you have it climb back down. Keep in mind, you're getting further into the castle now, so the guards are going to become much more serious.

Use the Spark Pylon to go to the third courtyard just to the side of the one you're in. Go to the next battlement using the Spark Pylon, grab the Warp Flag and then head up the stairs in front of you. Just make sure to avoid the Spinies while doing all this!

The Staircase Ogre will be to your right as you go up the stairs resting on a platform. These ogres will try to stomp on Mario every time he is around. Dodge the stomping and take note of the staircase that comes down each time the ogre stomps. You need to ground pound him, take your Power Moon and then double jump to grab the ladder and go right up it.

BOWSER RAMPS UP HIS DEFENSES

Bowser knows that Mario is getting closer, and he will do all he can to get rid of him. In this next level, the bombs will rain down upon you, so prepare for the worst.

You will end up in the second courtyard, where you'll notice many cannonball bombs released by Turrets falling down around you. Pokios will start coming around when this happens, but by capturing one, you can actually deflect the hit of the ball. They can turn the bombs around and shoot them back at the sender.

The first turret has a broken shard of Power Moon that must be put together in order to stop the madness. It was made this way so that intruders could not just come in and stop the destruction from happening. To gather these pieces, you just have to look in each of the following places:

· Under the first turret

· Hovering in front of the wall

· Over the fire pit

· Hidden in one of the bomb boxes between two of the turrets

· Tucked up on a ledge towards the back of the structure

Once the Power Moon is put together, you can open up the doors to the gate that reveals a Spark Pylon for Mario to ride down to the next level.

TIME FOR ANOTHER BATTLE

You're going to have to take on two of the bosses again when you come to the next room. Make sure to rest and relax before this fight, so you can go through both and come out the winner. Stop by the shop or relax by the comfortable woods to prepare.

Hariet is the first boss you're going to come against. You have already fought her before, so you should be somewhat familiar with what's to come. Go through the two golden Bowser statues to get to her. She'll throw her pigtail bombs right at you as soon as she hops from the ship above, so be prepared.

You will want to deflect and dodge the bombs as much as you can but it's not an easy task. She's relentless and is going to keep throwing them until you make her stop. Use a ground pound to jump on her head. She'll throw a fit when you do, but keep fighting and use Cappy to remove the hat from her head so you can beat her once and for all.

Repeat the cycle a few times in order to defeat her. When you do, another boss is standing there ready to take you on.

Topper is the next boss you're going to meet in this battle arena. You just have to step to the right of the platform to have him come out and start the next fight.

Always stay your distance from Topper because his Top Hat does damage in a short radius around him. His attacks often come without warning, but you'll be safe as long as you maintain a decent range from the boss.

Use Cappy to knock the stack of hats off his head. Keep up your attack until all of the hats are off. This is the only to get him open in order for Mario to beat him. Be ready with a ground pound assault the moment his head is free from his many hats. Just be mindful of the top hats that are going to try to stop you. Jump on them, dodge them and use Cappy to knock them out of the way.

Once you beat both of the bosses, you can easily grab the Power Moon and head to the next quest. You have to find Bowser!

BOWSER'S CASTLE, AT LAST!

Once you're done with those battles, you will be able to see Bowser's Castle straight ahead as you walk out of the gates. Grab the checkpoint in this area as you walk through and then head on to the castle. Rely on your binoculars to see what is happening up ahead of you and travel with care to avoid most of the danger.

Grab a Pokio and use it to climb the sides of the walls that extend to the outside of the platform. You'll quickly gain respect for the Pokio's climbing ability in this situation.

On the top of this wall, there will be skinny bridges that meet with one another. While crossing watch for the cannonballs coming from the turrets since they randomly shoot out, causing Mario to have to dodge on these skinny bridges. Whenever you're in danger and dodging isn't an option, your captured Pokio can send away the cannonballs using its beak.

Find the outer wall checkpoint as you follow the path. Grab the regional coins right in this area, as well.

This next task will take on a whole new level of game play. You're about to take on a two stage climbing wall that you have to get over with an ogre and moat down below it. Use the rotating disc that the ogre is wearing to move upward. Make sure to collect as many coins as you can on your way up.

Alternate on the conveyer belts that come and go to get across this level. The lighter colored sections of the wall can be pierced by the Pokio's beak but the other sections cannot. Move behind the spike strip on the left and you can gather some regional coins.

The last checkpoint that you're going to come across is behind a second run of obstacles stuck to a wall. Cross over the poison moats to the platform and then use the Spark Pylon to go to the roof of Bowser's Keep. However, it is not Bowser that Mario is up against. You get to meet with Koopa King instead.

Many of the members of Bowser's following have joined forces inside a major mechanical beast in order to take down Mario. It's able to stomp down on Mario, send out cannonballs and even spawn ground slithering snakes. Sometimes, the beast will use Pokios to help him, but this can work in your favor since Mario can capture them and then use them to deflect the cannonballs.

Sending just one cannonball crashing into the beast can get the armor off of it. Crash them into the legs of the beast to have it fall down. You will have to knock the Robo beast down at least four times, since you need to be able to break the four globes that are sitting atop its head.

Make sure to watch for a glowing light from the beast, as this signals that it is about to charge back and forth. When that happens make sure that Mario is well out of the way or it's all over with. This mechanical monster will become even more angry with each blow that he takes, causing him to change up his attack and become more difficult to defeat.

Ground pounding the globes, breaking all four and defeating this Robo beast brings on a Power Moon that you can collect at the end of the battle.

- 100 regional currency coins can be found throughout Bowser's Kingdom. You can check for them around the edges of structures and above doorways that you go into or pass.

- Bowser's Kingdom also has 62 Power Moons hidden within the walls of the fortress. You have to earn some of them through battles and quests, but you can also find them hidden throughout the castle in hidden corridors, under floors, in crates and in treasure chests hidden around the castle.

MOON KINGDOM

020

HONEYLUNE RIDGE

Just like a moon is what you can expect from this kingdom. It is dark and glowing and everything has a gray color to it. It is also one of those places that you don't know much about. You do know that it is your next stop to finding Bowser though, so you have to continue along.

THE MOON KINGDOM IS NOT WITHOUT QUESTS FOR MARIO

Bowser is hoping for a moon wedding and when you arrive, you can see the Wedding Hall right off in the distance. Of course it's your number one priority to stop the wedding, since Princess Peach isn't interested in being stuck with Bowser forever. You'll be fighting through a series of challenges on the way to this goal though.

ZERO GRAVITY, BETTER JUMPS

Since this kingdom is not as large as the others, you want to do your best to play through the end of it on your own. Find the hidden regional coins, as well as the Power Moons to complete the mission here. Of course, keep in mind that any jumps you make will be much higher than normal since gravity is very low here.

Start your trip going down each of the pathways and be careful to grab the checkpoints as you go along. These are important in case you run across something particularly nasty that will take you out.

THOSE MOON CAVERNS ARE UNDERGROUND

Drop down below the platform where you'll get your gravity back. You will also be in an area that is hot and has lava, so keep that in mind. As soon as you can, capture one of the Parabones that are flying about. They're going to help you fly over the lava lakes much more quickly than you could do on your own.

While questing you'll find cages with locked items inside. To open them up you just have to capture a Sherm and blast the cages apart and gather the items within. You need to open the Spark Pylon cage in order to advance to the next level, but grabbing the life-up heart is beneficial, too!

Ride the Spark Pylon and slap the big red button that awaits you at the end of the ride. Your platform will start to move and you will see Hammer Bros. Capture one of these since you will need to use their rain of hammers in order to break through the way ahead.

Ground pound the second red button that you get to and this will get the next platform moving to the next stop. Capture a Tropical Wiggler to use as you journey to the next area. You will want to use them to collect the coins you see along the way. Once you're at the end, you can ditch the Wiggler and move on.

You will notice that Banzai Bill is demolishing the walls ahead and barreling down the bridge, right towards you! Use two cap throws to capture him and then ride him over the lava and the platforms ahead.

Once you get into the room, ground pound the red button to get the platform moving to the next area. When you start moving, you can try to grab the regional coins that are there by reaching out or throwing your cap in their direction.

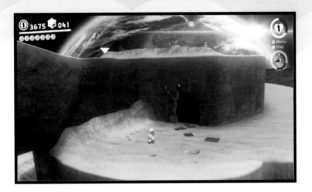

Keep your eyes open since the Moe-Eye's hidden bridge is where you're going to be crossing and when you get to the other side, prepare for a showdown with another one of the bosses that come to play. You want to run along the rocks and the bridges, capture Chuck and then hold onto him so that you can use his dash to get over the rocks and crevices that you come across in the road. These tiny gaps can cost you your life, so using the dash power helps you quickly move over them. Just make sure to watch out for any oncoming rocks.

Go up and almost all of the way out of the cavern, then jump onto the next Spark Pylon.

Using the Pylon brings you face to face with Madame Broode once again and she is just as angry as she was before. Just like you had to do before, you have to dodge her chains that she sends out, while also knocking her hats off her head with Cappy. Once the hat is off, ground pounding her can help you defeat her. Keep this momentum going. You'll have to go through the steps a few more times to win.

Of course, once you do, she is just going to run off back to the lunar surface and take off on her spaceship!

TIME TO CRASH THE BIG WEDDING

At last! You have arrived in the right place, at the right time and you are dressed to impress! Make sure to grab the checkpoint before moving forward!

Head on up to the Wedding Hall where you're sure to find everyone ready for the day's festivities, or what they think are going to be festival-like! Once you go through the main entrance of the hall, go off to the right to crack open a rock and grab the life-up heart, since you may need it!

Enter the foyer of the Wedding Hall and then barge through the front doors of the room.

BOWSER IS NOT GOING TO GIVE UP

Bowser wants Princess Peach so when you go through those doors, he is not going to just give her up to you. He's going to put up the fight of his life to keep her by his side, and he has a few new tricks up his sleeve too!

Just like the last fight, you can expect to find the series of hats that you've come to know. You'll also have a white hat as a target once again. To win the fight Mario will have to capture the white hat and then use it against Bowser while also dodging the other hats down on the ground.

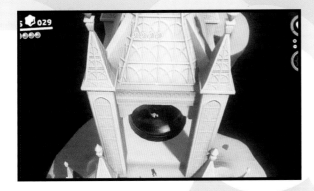

One thing that Bowser is going to do differently though, is that he will send flames shooting out to cover the ground. Mario must be quick and jump over them before getting burned! Bowser then resorts to using boulders and cannonballs to try and stop Mario. However, Mario can break apart the boulders and the cannonballs can easily be jumped over or dodged. You just have to make sure that Mario is very agile and patient throughout this entire fight.

Watch out for Bowser's tail whip as he tries to take Mario out. Jumping over it is the most effective way to avoid the attack. Make Mario punch Bowser as much as possible in the face, this is the way to win. With each tail swipe, Mario can catch him on his way back around. With careful timing you can completely take control of the fight without taking much damage at all. Bowser will keep trying to tail whip Mario, but repeatedly punching him will bring him down before long.

AND THEN THE ESCAPE...

Winning three waves against Bowser can result in a victory for Mario. However, once the castle around them starts to shake and collapse, a route out of there is required. If no one is able to find a way out, this can mean that everyone might parish along with the building!

A breakable stone wall will appear and Mario will have to destroy it. Shake the controller to do so. This causes a fireball to be released into the wall, breaking it down, giving Mario an escape route. Just make sure to watch for boulders that will be falling down all around you.

Go to the main room from the escape tunnel. You will notice four pillars set up there. Dismantle each of the four pillars, but watch out as you do so, since you don't want anything from above falling down on you. Take them all out and then Cappy will let you know that the central block is now vulnerable.

Run to the center and focus all of your attacks on that one block.

- 50 Regional Coins can be found throughout the walls of this kingdom, so keep an eye out for them as you move along in your journey. Look under shallow bridges, in cannons and in the Wedding Hall.

- Only 38 Power Moons are hidden throughout this region, keep an eye out for them, with some of the areas not holding any at all. Check along the cliff face, in the rolling rocks all over the moon's surface, up in the rafters or even with the art.

MUSHROOM KINGDOM

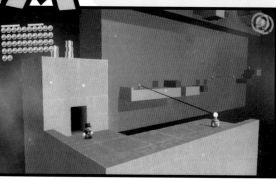

PEACH'S CASTLE

Peach's Castle is where she calls home, so it is no wonder it is a place you're going to go to next. With many things happening all at once, the people of the region want to know what happened to their Princess and how they're able to get her back! Don't worry though, Mario is here to save Princess Peach and the day!

This whole chapter is mostly finding Power Moons for fun and exploring the area. You can make the most of this kingdom when you go and run around. Find out what each area has to offer! You might be surprised at where some of the items are hiding right in Mario's own home town!

PRINCESS PEACH'S REGION HAS A JOB FOR MARIO

What kind of kingdom would this be if they did not ask Mario for a bit of his help? Mario still calls this kingdom his home and the townsfolk are just as happy as ever to see him and want to tell him of everything that has happened since he has been gone.

Check the castle to make sure Peach is still there and doing good and that she survived everything that has happened before. Of course, Peach and Tiara have already packed up by the time that you arrive, so you are going to have to come back again to see them.

TIPS

- Find up to 100 regional coins hidden throughout the kingdom. Look up on the top of towers, in the tunnels below and those hovering over the drop offs.

- There are also 43 Power Moons hidden throughout the lands, so you want to check in many places. This is after all the only objective that this kingdom has for Mario to take on. Check out Peach's Castle, around the well and in the flower garden.

Head off to another kingdom?   Set Sail   Cancel

With so much happening in Mario Odyssey, there is so much more that can be said. We're sure you have found your own tips and tricks and created a strategy of your own to get through many of the areas. However, use our guide to help you get past some of the trickier areas that you come across.

You never know when you might be able to benefit from a helping hand along the way. Don't worry about failing a bit before you succeed, that's exactly how you'll make it through the tougher parts of the game.

Remember, just because you collected over 500 Power Moons does not mean you're done. There are literally hundreds more Power Moons waiting for you to collect them. You just have to journey back to where you started and keep adding to the amount. Use the numbers provided above to count down the ones you have and the ones that are still left to find. That is the whole fun of the game — and beating Bowser!

Now it's time to get started on your journey, through the kingdoms and to allow Mario to have some jump time. He's come a long way, but he's always ready to rescue Princess Peach, and he'll have to work harder than ever before to succeed in Mario Odyssey.

If you think you have what it takes to succeed in the game, go out there and try to beat Bowser. Just make sure to stop every now and then to enjoy the worlds, to enjoy the townsfolk and enjoy all that the game has to offer, including the Cap Shops along the way that can provide some pretty sweet gear.

BEAT THE BOSS, RESCUE THE PRINCESS AND TAKE OFF INTO THE SUNSET!

HOW TO REV UP YOUR MARIO KART LIVE EXPERIENCE

The super innovative Mario Kart Live: Home Circuit game for the Nintendo Switch system allows you to race Mario and Luigi mini karts through courses you make in your home!

The onus is on you to be creative when setting up your course based on the space and any items you have available, while the racing appears on your screen via augmented-reality technology (like Pokémon Go).

The only thing you must use in your course are four cardboard gates that are provided with your kart, to give the tech some orientation in your course. Whether you live in a castle like Peach or a studio apartment, here are some ideas to help you get the most out of this clever and charming title.

MAKE FURNITURE INTO MOUNTAINS

When planning your first Mario Kart Live: Home Circuit track, consider the layout of your room. Even if it's small (and we'll get to that later) you probably have some furniture. Pull a couch or bed or cabinet a few inches from the wall so the karts can fit behind it and voila, you have created a mountain pass.

FACTOR IN FRICTION

While the karts are designed to scoot on just about any flooring, if you have an option for a hard surface such as vinyl or wood try to build a course there—or at least incorporate as much of it as you can into a larger course. The cars will literally run longer because of less friction between the tires and the track on a hard surface as opposed to carpet.

CREATE YOUR OWN HOME CIRCUIT

Whether you have limited space or not, explore different areas where you can set up courses. Kitchens can make great courses as they're usually a hard surface flooring and if you have an island or kitchen table and chairs, all the better! Pots, pans, and small appliances also make for great visuals and track props. That said, open hallways and even bedrooms, can make great courses with a little imagination and say, a stack of pillows as obstacles.

BECOME A MAPMAKER

While you can certainly just build your course freestyle, and indeed you and friends can even make course design part of your competition, it helps to craft a plan and fine-tune your course with a few practice runs. When you create a track keep it simple at first—you can always go back and add length, turns, and shortcuts. Once you are familiar with the course, angles of turns and timing, add an obstacle, tunnel,

or straightaway and see how it impacts the drivers before making it a permanent part of your race course.

CREATE COOL THEMED SCENES

Are you a doll or dinosaur nut, or does someone you know have a cool Lego, sports memorabilia, or horror collection? Then you already have the makings of an awesome track, friend! You can make a hilarious and customized course out of stuff you or your friends and family are interested in. It's a great way to raise the stakes and make the Mario Kart Live experience uniquely personal. You can also build tracks around seasonal themes such as Christmas, Halloween, Fourth of July, etc.

ALL IN ALL, IT'S ABOUT THE WALLS

It helps for navigation and in creating a sensation of speed if your track has walls to keep drivers corralled. Use anything you can find, from furniture, to shoes, to books, backpacks, cardboard—anything light and solid than can help you mark the course clearly. Also keep in mind neither the game nor your NPC competitors can actually "see" your course so it is better to keep it somewhat conventional, or you will find them zipping straight though spots that your physical karts won't fit.

SUPER MARIO MAKER 2

Super Mario Maker 2 is a virtual toolbox of game mechanisms that allows you to create your own levels of a video game using blocks, power ups, and enemies from Super Mario history. And the best part? You can share levels through Nintendo Switch Online and also play, rate, and download levels made by other players!

While multiplayer levels can be played locally without all players having a Nintendo Switch Online membership, it does require at least one player to have a Nintendo Switch Online subscription and be connected to the internet. One connected player can make a virtual room for any three nearby players to

join—as long as they have their own Nintendo Switch and Super Mario Maker 2 game.

An all-new Story Mode is a highlight of this sequel, which features over 100 familiar and yet different levels created by the masters at Nintendo to test your skills, and cleverly teach you a thing or two.

In this guide we'll teach you how to unlock Story Mode characters for secret levels and rewards; show you how to unleash exclusive power-ups for use in your own creations; and even rebuild Princess Peach's castle.

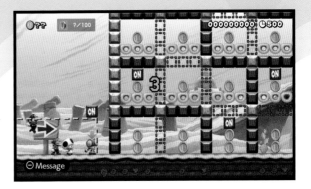

MULTIPLAYER

The Course World is the mecca for multiplayer mode. Here, you'll search for levels, view leaderboards, go online, and play the Endless Challenge mode. Endless Challenge allows you to play an infinite stream of randomized levels.

PRO TIP: Any extra lives you collect carry over to the next level. How many can you accumulate?

You can also download any of the levels you encounter in this mode, and even edit them. This is also the place where you can upload any levels you've made.

HOW TO PLAY ONLINE MULTIPLAYER

Selecting the Network Play option in Course World gives you access to Global Play, which allows you to engage in the action with three other players in either Co-op or Versus mode.

Your player gets rated after finishing the level, and your score is dependent on a variety of factors like how long it took you to complete the level, how cleanly you completed the level, and how many coins and points you earned in the level. Your rating results in Maker Points, and the better you do, the more Maker Points you'll earn.

PRO TIP: Your Versus ranking also reflects your performance and adjusts accordingly as you play. You'll be matched with players of similar rank in Versus play.

Meanwhile, Co-op matches are not scored at the end. Once one player completes the level, the whole team succeeds.

4 PLAYERS

Four players can play Super Mario Maker 2 on one screen. All offline levels are playable this way as long as each player has their own controller. Respawns work like they do in the New Super Mario Bros. U games, where you respawn inside a bubble that a teammate has to pop to reactivate you.

The course editor also supports two players on the same screen, allowing you and a mate to build and edit levels together.

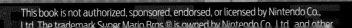

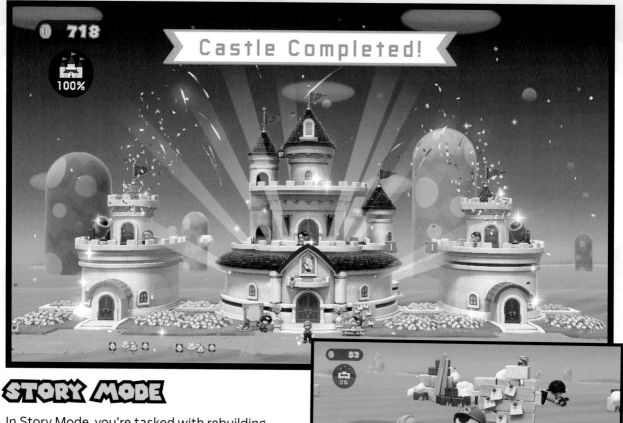

STORY MODE

In Story Mode, you're tasked with rebuilding Princess Peach's Castle. A series of jobs must be completed in sequence for you to earn coins for the castle's reconstruction. Jobs are broken down into levels you must complete, and your rewards are coins and hammers for building.

More than 100 levels introduce you to the mechanics and concepts of level design. Levels showcase and demonstrate many of the nifty elements you can eventually use in your designs, and provide insight into how many of the structures and mechanics may be implemented.

Your percentage completion of the castle's reconstruction is displayed on the left side of the screen. As you rebuild the castle, you'll encounter more characters offering you more levels to complete. Levels will become more difficult and complex as you progress through the Story Mode.

PRO TIP: You can always go back and complete levels that you've already solved if you need to replenish your supplies.

After completing the first level, you'll have enough coins to begin work on the Foundation. Coins and hammers are the key commodities you need to build-out each level. As you progress through this linear building process, each structure unlocks a new phase of the castle build.

Here's the cost of each SMM2 structure and which levels they unlock:

Structure	Coin Cost	Hammers Required	Levels Unlocked
Foundation	100	2	5 - 6
Main Hall 1F	600	4	7 - 9
West Hall 1F	400	3	10 - 12
East Hall 1F	400	3	13 - 15
Main Hall 2F	1200	4	16 - 21

After completing the Main Hall 2F, speak with Red Toad and complete his level to get access to build 3F.

After completing the Main Hall 2F and West Hall 1F, speak with Green Toad and complete his level to get access to build West Hall 2F.

After completing the Main Hall 2F and East Hall 1F, speak to Blue Toad and complete his level to get access to build East Hall 2F.

Structure	Coin Cost	Hammers Required	Levels Unlocked
Main Hall 3F	1300	5	22 - 27
West Hall 2F	1100	4	28 - 33
East Hall 2F	1100	4	34 - 39

After completing Main Hall 3F, speak with the Task Master to complete his Toad Rescue level to continue construction.

Structure	Coin Cost	Hammers Required	Levels Unlocked
West Hall Cannon	700	4	40 - 44
West Hall Doors	500	3	46 - 50
East Hall Cannon	700	4	51 - 55
East Hall Doors	500	3	56 - 61
Main Hall Roof	1500	5	62 - 68
West Hall Roof	1000	4	69 - 75
East Hall Roof	1000	4	76 - 82

Once you're done building all structures, the Stained-Glass Portrait becomes available.

Structure	Coin Cost	Hammers Required	Levels Unlocked
Stained Glass	2000	5	83 - 90

Each level is ranked in difficulty from 1 (easiest) to 4 (hardest) and the payment for conquering each level is reflected accordingly.

For example, the first time you complete a level you get 100 coins; the second time, 150 coins; the third, 200 coins; and the fourth and most difficult passage will earn you a whopping 300 coins! These bonus rewards are received the first time you complete each level. While replaying a level will not give you the bonus payouts a second time, you can keep any coins you gathered within the level.

PRO TIP: Reaching the top of the Flagpole at the end of a level earns you 10 extra coins, every time!

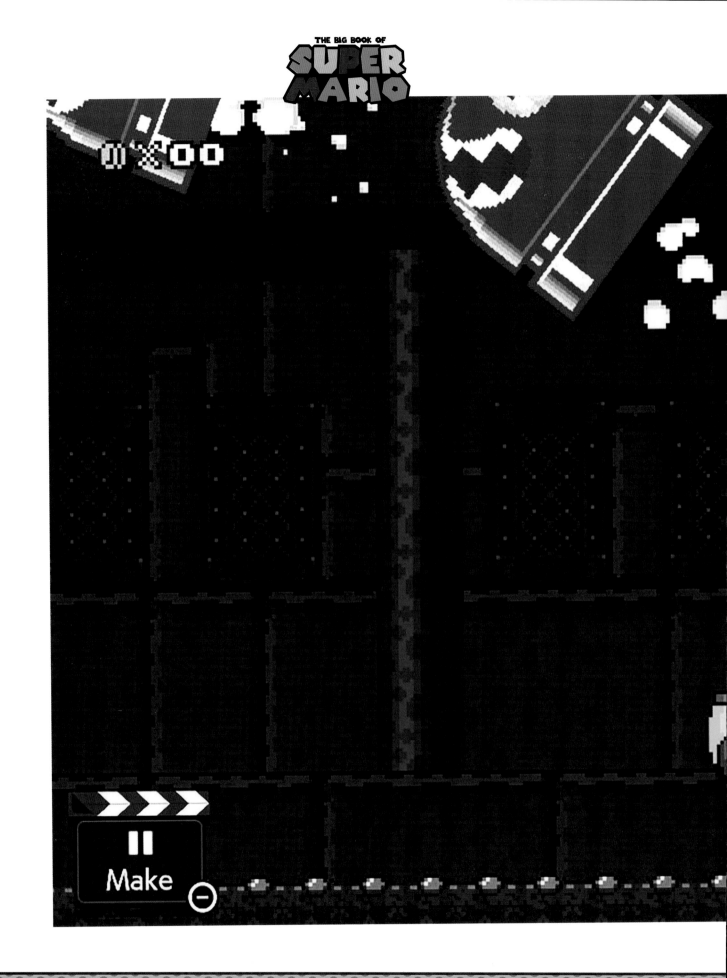

00000000 ⏱288

Mr. Eraser

If you ever need something...removed from the equation, just call on Mr. Eraser. Adios...

Partrick

Hello.
Have time for a job?

CHARACTERS

Story Mode introduces you to a wonderful cast of colorful characters—some legendary and some not-so-familiar—you'll encounter in the Mario Maker universe. Characters with a red exclamation mark above their heads indicate they have a specific job to do, and you should engage them by pressing A to interact. Once you do, their level will be available for implementation. After completing the job, you will be awarded coins or custom threads or gear for your Mii Maker Profile.

MR. ERASER

As you build the Main Hall 1F, Mr. Eraser will appear on the right side of the road. He offers to clear out the blocks impeding the Warp Pipe and eventually those on the Road. When he has a red exclamation mark above his head, talk to him to unlock his job.

PARTRICK

Once you complete Mr. Eraser's first job, hop into the green Warp Pipe and descend to the area below and walk to the right to interact with the brick, where you'll find Partrick. Speak with him and he'll add a bunch of blocks to your building stash.

PURPLE TOAD

After completing the second floor of the Main Hall, speak with Red Toad and help him on a search and rescue mission for Purple Toad. After completing the job, Purple Toad can be found on the east side of the road next to the sleepy Yellow Toad. Finishing all of Purple Toad's jobs will unlock the cool Superball Flower power-up.

SOUNDFROG

After completing Partrick's second job, Soundfrog becomes available by approaching the red flower and jumping to activate the hidden block. When the vine emerges press A to jump on it and climb up. When you reach the cloud go left, collect the coins, and talk to Soundfrog. He boasts some of the toughest levels for you to get through, but once you do the entire landscape transforms!

PRO TIP: Once you're done with his levels try speaking with Soundfrog to get him to dance.

UNDODOG

When the West Hall is near competition, the Undodog will not-so-pleasantly start barking jobs at you. All these jobs require clear conditions and get progressively more difficult. You snag some cool, new threads after completing all three jobs.

Yellow Toad

I couldn't get my hands on the Stone that the Chief wanted, so I took a nap instead.

Ⓐ

YELLOW TOAD

On the east side of the road, near those huge blocks you can see, you'll find a dozing Yellow Toad. When he wakes up, he'll offer you jobs that require clear conditions and revolve around grabbing stones. When you complete his jobs, you unlock a fancy statue for decoration.

YAMAMURA

When you fire the West Hall Cannon the first time, Yamamura will land on the left side of the road between the floating blocks and the newly-built Undodog house. You need to keep tabs on Yamamura, which is easier said than done, to complete the next two jobs.

After handling Yamamura's jobs, talk to Red Toad on the 2nd floor of the Main Hall and you'll learn about an ON/OFF switch installed on the 3rd floor. You have to jump to flip the switch and once you do, Yamamura will pop-out like a coo-coo clock bird. If you continue flicking the switch Yamamura will appear with different poses and may have other surprises in store!

POWER-UPS AND UNLOCKABLES

Two major power-ups can be unlocked by playing through Story Mode. Here's how to unlock them:

#1 SUPER HAMMER: BUILDER MARIO

After you complete Peach's Castle in Story Mode, you unlock Mario's mighty Super Hammer to wield in Course Maker mode. The Super Hammer whomps Mario into Builder Mario, and allows him to make his own Builder Boxes and all the goodness that springs from them. In Multiplayer Mode each character's Builder Box features their signature color and custom emblem.

PRO TIP: You can spawn no more than five boxes. If you try and make a sixth, the first box vanishes. That said, with four players you can spawn 20 boxes!

By swinging his hammer, Builder Mario can bust blocks and pummel predators. Here's a roster of stuff BM can bop with one swing of his mighty mallet!

- **Block**
- **? Block**
- **Ice Block**
- **Crates**
- **Hop-Chop**
- **Dry Bones**
- **Lava Bubble**
- **Peepa**

- **Hard Block**
- **Hidden Block**
- **Icicle**
- **Spiny**
- **Thwomp**
- **Fish Bones**
- **Boo**

#2 SUPERBALL FLOWER: SUPERBALL MARIO

You unlock this coveted tool in Story Mode after completing the Spiny Shell Smashers job. Purple Toad will destroy the hard blocks below the row of three floating question mark blocks. Once PT handles his business, jump up and knock the middle question mark block to unlock the Superball Flower.

The Superball Flower will now be available in the Course Maker. This power-up transforms Mario into Superball Mario. Superball Mario can destroy enemies by pressing Y to shoot, but he can only shoot one superball at a time. The upside is that the superballs have a much greater velocity than fireballs and also bounce off surfaces, giving them a much more potent punch.

Builder Mario Complete!

100%

PRO TIP: Superballs also pump-up the music after Mario transforms!

AFTER STORY MODE: JOBS AND SECRETS

Though you might think you're done after completing Story Mode, there's still a lot of work to do!

Building Peach's Castle required you to complete about two-thirds of the Taskmaster's jobs, and now is a great time to go back and finish any levels you've missed, and scour your levels and jobs checklists more thoroughly:

PRINCESS PEACH'S JOBS

Check-in with the Taskmaster to get your jobs from Princess Peach. The very first level calls for your Super Hammer, which is awesome. As you complete each of her jobs you obtain cool new duds for your Mii in your Maker Profile.

CHIEF TOADETTE AND THE BUILDER MARIO STATUE

Chief Toadette teases that she can build you something awesome for 1,000 Coins, and let's just say you won't be disappointed. When you give her the Coins the base of a statue will be constructed to the left of the West Hall. It cost an additional 1,000 Coins to build each part of the statue, and the statue is composed of ten parts. Speaking with Chief Toadette can keep you appraised of the construction progress.

Coursebot

Beep boop.
(Hello, Mario.)

Ⓐ

COURSEBOT

Coursebot—a smallish red bulb sticking out of the ground—can be found in the underground section accessed by the Warp Pipe on the far west edge of the road. It's easy to miss at first since it was blocked earlier by a Piranha Creeper.

If you haven't cleared the Creeper yet, you need to talk to Purple Toad and handle that job, known as Piranha Creeper Squash, first. The Warp Pipe gives you access to the area underground, so descend through it and you'll be able to break the blocks.

At the end of the passageway lies the lower half of Coursebot. Jump repeatedly underneath to help break it through the ground above. Once you do, go back above grade and engage Coursebot. Interacting with Coursebot allows you to enjoy Story Mode cutscenes for the Intro, Ending, and Credits.

MARIO MOVES

Mario has many famous and familiar moves he has become known for through the decades, and most but not all of them have found their way into this game. Certain moves and abilities are restricted to certain game styles, so pay attention to what you can or can't do based on what sorts of levels and content you're trying to design.

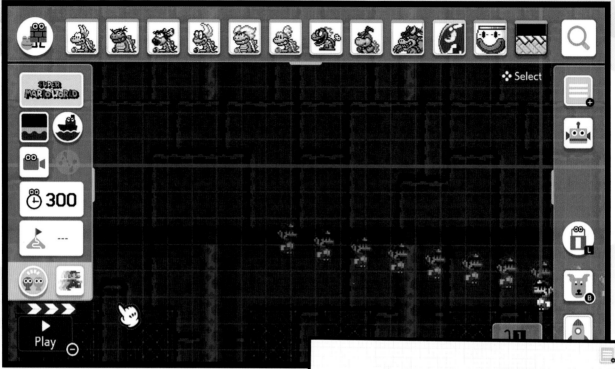

RESOURCES

No doubt about it, SMM2 is a broad and complicated "game." Nintendo knows this and has thoughtfully embedded some useful tools and resources to help you get the most out of this slick software:

MAKER BASICS

The Maker Basics tutorial is most useful for those who have no idea what this game is about, while Yamamura's Dojo provides more nuanced information and detail for experienced creators. There are three sets of lessons—Beginner, Intermediate, and Advanced—composed of 15 videos each, so there is a lot of content for you to absorb. These videos basically teach you how to become a video game level designer by showing you how to more effectively deploy game mechanisms and pacing in your levels.

YAMAMURA'S DOJO

Tutorials can be found in Yamamura's Dojo which you can visit by going to the Main Menu and selecting the pigeon icon at the bottom of the screen. While we understand you want to get to the fun part and build your own levels, the time you spend watching videos will save you a ton of time learning these things by trial and error on your own.

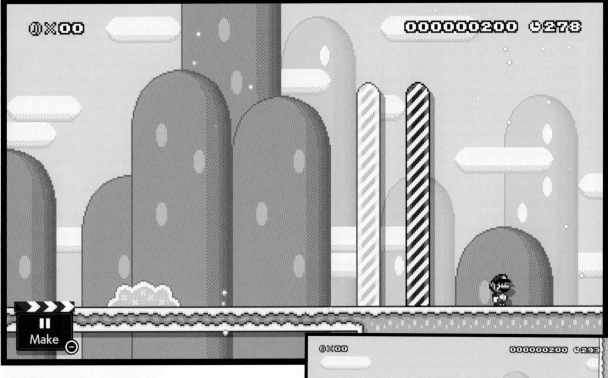

BUILDER TIPS

START SIMPLE

While it may be tempting to want to dive right in and start designing complex 3D worlds, we strongly advise you to plan to make your first level basic. The Game Style you choose determines Mario's moves and capabilities, and it's best to start simple as you embark on the learning curve.

Design the type of level you enjoy playing. For example, if you want a level that emphasizes wall-jumping skills, you should build your level using the New Super Mario Bros. U style. Keep in mind that each Game Style has its own challenges, features, and power-ups. Building a level that is in sync with the mechanics of that style will result in a more cohesive gameplay experience.

CRAFTING CLEAR CONDITIONS

Clear Conditions are specific tasks and goals players must complete before reaching the Flagpole at the end of your level. Whether you set up your level so that a player has to collect X number of coins, or vanquish a particular enemy or enemies, the level can't be beaten if your Clear Condition is not met.

Clear Conditions can help you funnel players through your level and have the experience you want them to have, instead of having them speed-run through your level with challenge or exploration.

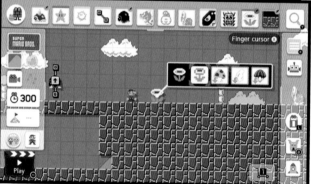

PRO TIP: Cleverly crafted Clear Conditions should be tricky enough to make some folks who play your level get stuck, but not so difficult that people get frustrated and quit trying.

STORY MODE CONTAINS UNLOCKABLE POWERUPS

Remember the two Mario transformations that you should have unlocked by now in Story Mode? Now you can make use of them, but don't forget one is exclusive to the Super Mario 3D World style, and the other is exclusive to the Super Mario Bros. style.

TRY A STYLUS

This game features a lot of intricate manipulation, so we recommend trying a stylus for more granular control of your touchscreen and tools.

NIGHT MODE (MOON) ROCKS!

Perhaps the niftiest new feature of SMM2 is Night Mode. All you have to do is place a Moon in your level and it can literally transform your level into a spectacularly cool, colorful, and slightly different experience than what you originally created. The difference a Moon makes is like night and day! We'll venture further into Night Mode later in this article.

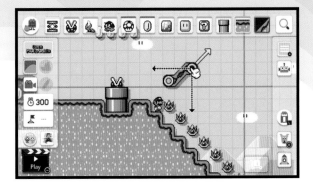

UPLOADING LEVELS: DEFEAT YOUR OWN CREATIONS

Once your ideal level is complete, use the Coursebot to save it and give it a test run! You must be able to clear your own level in order to upload it. Of course, you're biased about your freshly minted content, but try to take a step back and determine if people will find it fun or not.

Once you pass the test, you can write a brief description for your level, and choose two descriptor Tags to make it searchable for others. A catchy name and fun or irreverent theme will definitely make your level more appealing to others.

LEVEL DESIGN DO'S AND DON'TS

DON'T clown players with unrealistic asks. For example, don't ask players to make leaps of faith offscreen where they can't see where or how far they have to jump.

DO use the breadcrumb rule: steer players where you want them to go by using coins, arrows, and visual cues.

DON'T hide items that a player needs to complete a level in a random or illogical spot. If you try to get too tricky, people will eventually give up on your level.

DO consider locking the camera onto a certain area if you want the player to focus on something. It's a great way to give them a clue without making your surprise so obvious.

DON'T just try and pepper players with enemies everywhere. Consider the strengths and weaknesses of your enemy placement and try and maximize their threat with the use of obstacles and other contraptions that make them more lethal.

DO play through Story Mode, and then go play it again, to gather both obvious and subtle inspiration for your own creations and Clear Conditions.

DEEP DIVE ON CLEAR CONDITIONS

We already talked about the basics of Clear Conditions. If a player reaches the end of your level without completing your Clear Conditions, they will not see the flag pole.

A player can monitor their progress on this front via the top left corner of the screen. When Clear Conditions are met, a flag icon will appear next to Mario. There are three types of Clear Conditions: Actions, Parts, and Status.

ACTIONS (ALL GAME STYLES)

This Clear Condition requires the player to successfully perform a certain move or skill. Some basic Action Clear Conditions include:

- Reach the flag pole without taking any damage.

- Reach the flag pole without touching the ground once you leave it.

STATUS (BASIC GAME STYLES)

It's not how you start; it's how you finish when it comes to Status-based Clear Conditions. For example, these conditions require the player to reach the flag pole with a certain power-up or effect activated. Some conditions are only available in certain Game Styles so consider if and how you want your level to end in this way when you begin building your level.

PARTS (BASIC GAME STYLES)

Parts related Clear Conditions involve Mario's traditional collecting of items, or overcoming a spate of enemies. This is where you can really have some fun, as every item and enemy can be assigned a Clear Condition. Even the dreaded Munchers, which can only be defeated using a POW or Super Star Block, can be part of your onslaught—if you have gathered the materials to create them.

PARTS (SUPER MARIO 3D WORLD)

Super Mario 3D World boasts its own unique style and Clear Conditions that are exclusive to this title, while classic elements like coins and mushrooms are present. The theme matches the game that bears its title— Clear Conditions involve collecting a certain number of coins or taking down a preset number of enemies.

STATUS (SUPER MARIO 3D WORLD)

Since Super Mario 3D World is played from a unique perspective, it offers certain conditions that are unavailable in the other styles. Clear Conditions typically revolve around reaching the flag pole with a certain power-up or effect.

STORY MODE EXCLUSIVE CLEAR CONDITIONS

Story Mode has its own exclusive set of Clear Conditions that are not available in Course Maker. Here's a lineup of popular conditions:

Reach the end while holding a Stone type.
- **Stone of Destiny**
- **Heavy Stone Heave-Ho**
- **Buried Stones**
- **Cat-Scratch Stone**
- **Stone from the River**

Reach the end without using any Swinging Claws.
- **Swinging Claw Escape**

Reach the end without getting out of the water.
- **Hold Your Breath**

Reach the end with Toad in tow.
- **Little Toad Lost**
- **Toad Rescue**
- **Operation Toadal Eclipse**
- **March of the Rookie Toads**

Reach the end after traversing X number of trees.
- **Treetop Fireballs**
- **Master of the Trees**

NIGHT MODE

Night Mode makes everything cool, fresh and different, and it may be applied to every Course Theme in Super Mario Maker 2. Once you place the Angry Sun enemy in your level, all you have to do is tap it to turn it into the Moon.

Night Mode has all kinds of special effects on your content, some of which you can see and some you can't. For example, it transforms 1-up Mushrooms into Rotten Mushrooms, which means no extra lives for our hero in this mode. In fact, making contact with these 'shrooms will deal damage to Mario, and they're pesky enough to even follow your ascent through higher levels.

Other power-ups affected by Night Mode include:

Super Mushroom: Now bounces around randomly instead of moving steadily, and will even try to elude Mario.

Fire Flower: Now tries to jump or turn around to evade Mario.

(Super Mario Bros.) Big Mushroom: Bounces randomly and tries to avoid Mario.

(Super Mario Bros. 3) Tanooki Leaf: Flutters up and away from Mario.

(Super Mario World) Cape Feather: Falls to the ground much more rapidly.

(New Super Mario Bros. U) Propeller Mushroom: Spins haphazardly and then sputters out of reach.

THEMES AT NIGHT

Strange things happen when the sun goes down and the moon rules the sky. Here are some of the changes you can expect to see to the various game themes:

CASTLE (NIGHT)

Mario behaves like when he is underwater, which means you move in a swimming motion.

DESERT

Desolate sand storms seemingly whip up out of nowhere and blow through the level, while varying wind speeds and direction wreak havoc on tasks at hand.

FOREST

While it's darker in the trees at night it's the water that becomes a real menace, turning poisonous and dealing a death blow to anyone who touches it.

GHOST HOUSE (NIGHT)

A single spotlight illuminates Mario in a pitch-black setting, while fireballs provide a bit of peripheral vision. A Super Star can lighten things up.

000000000 🕐291

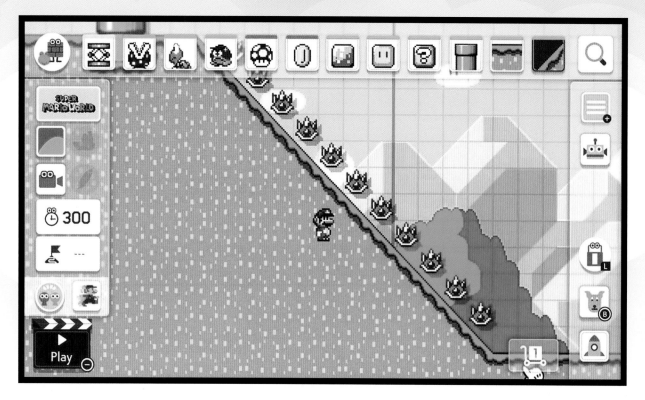

GROUND

The infamous Goombas float in air as if they're swimming underwater. Look out above and below!

SNOW

Another of our favorites, everything is made slippery by snow and ice. The name of the game is momentum and taking it slow, as too much velocity and too little stopping distance can spell trouble for your frigid friends.

SKY

With an effect that's akin to being on the Moon with much less gravity, players can get bigger air than ever with longer and higher jumps, and slower descents and falls. The catch is, enemies gain the same abilities, so float with caution.

UNDERGROUND

You might want to stand on your head for this one, as this level is literally upside down! While your right and left remain the same on screen, top and bottom are flipped. It takes a while to get your bearings in this simple but hilarious effect as you move up to go down slopes and down to ascend through obstacles.

UNDERWATER

One of our favorite effects, a lone spotlight shines on Mario in an otherwise murky screen. Try to locate and use a Super Star to make your world a little brighter.

Heya, big bro!
If you're having trouble with a course, use some assist parts!

LUIGI AS A LAST RESORT

Like so many memorable Mario moments through the years, if you find yourself stuck on a certain part of the game, you can count on li'l bro Luigi to come to the rescue!

Luigi will appear after you lose your second life, and offer some sibling assistance in two ways. He can help you edit your level by adding or removing elements or enemies to make things more bearable, or step in and complete the level for you.

Why not do that all the time, right?

The catch is, if Luigi helps you complete a level in any way, a Luigi flag is displayed next to the level on the Taskmaster's list (instead of a Mario flag) and while you will earn a reward for the course competition, you don't earn any extra coins.

You definitely want to try your best to do it yourself, but it's nice to know he's there to lend a helping hand.

MARIO PARTY SUPERSTARS
SURVIVAL AND VICTORY GUIDE

Nintendo finally released a Mario Party title that captures all of the appeal of the original titles from more than two decades ago, and updates it for the Switch and a new generation of fans, friends, and families. Here are some tips and info to get you jumpstarted on one of all-time great in-person multi-player party games!

CLASSIC CAST & GAME BOARDS

While there are no secret characters in Mario Party Superstars, the usual cast of favorites people love to play are, including Mario, Luigi, Princess Peach, Yoshi, Donkey Kong, Daisy, Wario, Waluigi, Rosalina, and Birdo. There are five remastered game boards from the classic N64 classic titles that spawned this series.

AN ASSIST FROM KING BOO

You can find the King Boo statue on the Horror Land board in the top right, blocked by a gate that requires a Skeleton Key. If you can pass by it at night (it must be night time to activate) and have 15 coins, it will snatch coins from all opponents for you, or even steal Stars if you have 150 coins!

GO FOR THE GOLD (PIPES, THAT IS)

Buy all the Golden Pipes you can. They cost 25 coins but it's basically like buying stars. Using one instantly whisks you away to the next star from wherever you are on the board. The best time to use a Golden Pipe is when an opponent is about to claim a star. You can swoop in right before their next move and snatch the Star, and leave them stuck on the map empty handed as the next star spawns at a new location.

ALL ABOUT THE $

Strange but true, but when you get down to it Mario Party is all about accumulating coins, which buys you stars, and wins you the game in the final tally. So, the name of the game is to go all-out, all the time to win or place as high as you can on every mini-game. You can't control the random events that happen on the board, so focus on being the best you can be in mini-games and mitigate the risk.

MASSIVELY PLAY THE MINI-GAMES

Mario Party Superstars is built on the foundation of mostly charming mini-games. Some are skill based, some have purely random outcomes, and some are simply button-mushing-madness. Practice on these as one-off contests from the main menu—many offer fun little playing sessions in their own right. If you focus on a few that you enjoy playing the most, it will make you that much more formidable when squaring off with friends and family.

BE WHO YOU ARE

Like in other Mario games, the physics of the characters are reflected in their size. If you like a more physical and burly presence, then go with Donkey Kong. If you prefer a more nimble sort, which definitely comes in handy on many of the more frenetic mini-games, use Peach or Yoshi. Mario and Luigi still represent the best balance of attributes, which Wario and Waluigi offer slight tradeoffs in attributes for more size.

SUPER MARIO BROS. U DELUXE

Welcome to our New Super Mario Bros. U Deluxe Walkthrough! In this guide, we will provide you with hints, tips, and tricks to help you get more out of playing this classic title. We'll also show you how to uncover many of the secret spaces and chambers in the game, as well as how to find exclusive items.

This guide is designed to be useful for everyone from those who have never played or are not familiar with this title, to experienced players who may have forgotten some of the pivotal moments and fun parts of this game, or who perhaps didn't unlock all the cool surprises the first time they played.

In the New Super Mario Bros. U Deluxe, the Mushroom Kingdom is in peril yet again. It's up to Mario and his friends to save the day, and you must steer your characters through several levels, using your platforming skills to overcome many perils, obstacles, and enemies.

How many coins can you collect?

WORLD 1: ACORN PLAINS

In the first world of the game, you'll find yourself in a generally flat and open space with a few rolling hills and trees.

The defining characteristic of this world is the mighty Acorn Tree, which you can use to get a Super Acorn. Make sure to always be on the lookout for this power-up, as it comes in handy sooner than you think.

Here's how to start covering ground in World 1: Acorn Plains.

Acorn Plains — Fortress: Crushing Cogs Tower

Main piece of advice for this level is to use the Ice Flower to freeze the Dry Bones. This allows you to pass by them more easily. You can also use the Ice Flower to temporarily freeze Boom Boom, a formidable foe who can easily take you out with one hit. Alternate between freezing him and stomping on him three times in succession, to vanquish him once and for all.

1: ACORN PLAINS WAY

You can snag the Flying Squirrel Suit by jumping on the Waddlewings. The suit gives you the ability to glide and reach higher places than you could otherwise, so make this a priority.

Meanwhile, keep in mind that whether you are small or big Mario, you will get a Super Acorn when you gather all the red coins in time, so go with the size that fits your style best.

Finally, take advantage of capturing the wave of coins—it teaches you how to do gliding jumps and this manuever is useful later in the game.

3: YOSHI HILL

Yoshi can be found near the beginning of the level, so track him down straight away. He can help you get through this level with his voracious ability to eat Monty Moles or Berries that drop power-ups and even 1-ups!

In addition to helping you find good loot, Yoshi can also help you by capturing a Venus Fire Trap fireball and burn enemies with it.

2: TILTED TUNNEL

This level is filled with Piranha Plants, so make liberal use of fireballs from the fire flower to keep them curtailed.

When you arrive at a twin set of straight pipes, the left one contains a bonus area where you will find a "?" brick with a Fire Flower power-up. Smash the brick, grab the flower.

Use the Red Koopa Troopa's shell and smack the upper-right brick from below. This triggers a vine descend from above that will lead you to a secret area, with more bonus goodies.

At the end of the level, you'll find a warp pipe that leads to the level's hidden flagpole.

4: MUSHROOM HEIGHTS

Before you start this level with the word "heights" in it, equip your Flying Squirrel Suit. In fact, you can use Baby Yoshi with balloon capabilities for short periods so he can hover above-ground level as needed!

You can stick to any wall with ease if you get the Raccoon Suit. This capability will be useful in later levels, so keep your eye out for this cool power-up.

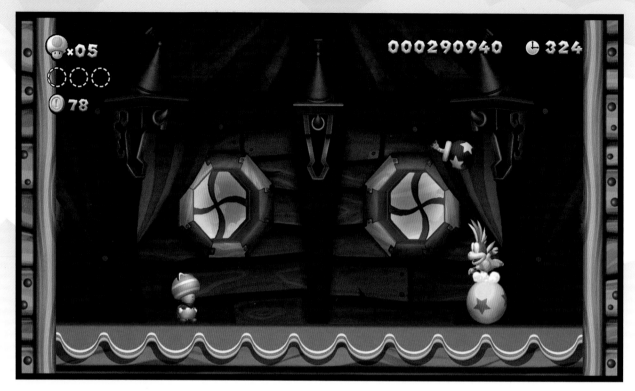

5: RISE OF THE PIRANHA PLANTS

You'll want to use Fire Mario at this level, so grab the first Fire Flower in a "?" block directly above your starting point.

Acorn Plains - Castle: Lemmy's Swingback Castle

Since this level is filled with lava that will kill you on contact, staying aloft by making use of the Flying Squirrel Suit is a sound strategy.

The first boss you encounter is Lemmy Koopa with his crushing ball. Stay nimble and keep dodging his attacks. It takes three stomps to defeat him.

Acorn Plains - Blooper: Blooper's Secret Lair

Using Fire Mario is best for this level, as his fireballs are effective against Bloopers and can help you dispatch them easier.

You will also notice that the currents of some pipes flow stronger than others and are harder to swim against, so adjust your timing and pipe choices accordingly.

WORLD 2: LAYER-CAKE DESERT

Layer-Cake Desert is the sandy second world of the game. It is located directly north of Acorn Plains, northwest of Sparkling Waters and Soda Jungle, and southwest of Frosted Glacier.

This tasty-looking world is based on a desert theme, with giant cakes, sweet treats, and dripping ice cream cones featured as some of the main obstacles in this level.

The boss of this world is Morton Koopa Jr., and he's no sweetheart.

1: STONE-EYE ZONE

Steer your character to the left of the palm trees and get on top of a stone head. Jump on it to hit an invisible block with an acorn.

As you scamper across the stone heads, watch out for those that sink or drift in different directions. They can throw off your timing and generally make your jumping more difficult.

2: PERILOUS POKEY CAVE

Use Fire Mario, or a Koopa shell to most effectively attack a Pokey's head and destroy it.

To clear tall Pokeys, make use of the sand geysers, but keep in mind they can also boost the Pokey's power as well.

When you encounter Swoopers you can only see the light from their eyes in the dimly lit cave. They are hard to sneak past and can deal serious damage, so keep an eye out for their piercing peepers.

3: FIRE SNAKE CAVERN

This level takes place in a forbidding cavern, but you will find it is fairly easy to navigate once you learn to rely on the light from Fire Snakes. The main thing here is to be prepared for when the Fire Snakes pop-up on you—they try to strike quickly before going back into hiding.

In this level, you can also gain access to more illumination by stepping on random platforms that light up, while enemy inhabitants release bursts of light when they are defeated.

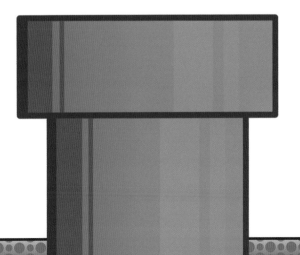

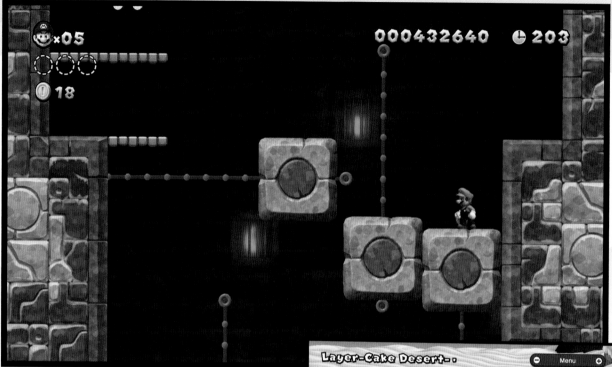

Here you should keep in mind that the yellow Yoshi is a great asset for both light and clearing out enemies. You can emit light sonars to illuminate the area as well as gobble down delicious enemies that are close enough so Yoshi's mouth can touch 'em—no need wasting time with ranged attacks!

Fortress: Stoneslide Tower
To get through this level, you have to use the Spin Jump to twist all the screws. Also keep in mind that platforms can be used as weapons against Dry Bones, so make the obstacles work for you.

The only way you can defeat Boom Boom is to stomp on him three times.

4: SPIKES SPOUTING SAND
The spiked ball the enemy throws at you is an easy target for converting into a power-up, if you can hit him from below.

PRO TIP: After getting the third Star Coin, drop down past the sign and go to the left to enter a secret exit that will whisk you to Piranha Plants on Ice!

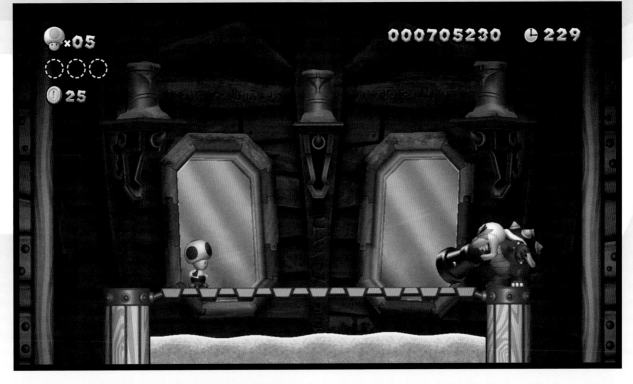

5: DRY DESERT MUSHROOMS

Be careful of the Stone Spikes that try to attack with their prickly parts. If you can survive them, you can find a powerup in the first "?" block.

6: BLOOMING LAKITUS

The Lakitus in this area is known for throwing eggs that turn into Piranha Plants. If you're able to kill them, their clouds become yours for the taking.

There is an Invincibility Star right before Star Coin #1 that can save you from taking damage, and you can also find an Ice Flower in the "?" brick below it.

Finally, if you're still packing a cloud, use it now to claim the bonus coins above the checkpoint at the end of the level.

Castle: Morton's Compactor Castle

The platforms on this level shift constantly, and can crush you between them if you're

not careful. You should also be mindful that Podobos can pop-up through the lava, so step lively!

This boss is different from previous titles. He does a Ground Pound that can stun your character if you are on the ground, and a giant Pokey rises from the sand following his attack.

When fighting Morton, it is important to not just avoid the segments of the Pokey he lobs at you using his hammer, but also taking care to not fall off the edge on your own, to your death.

Ice: Piranha Plants on Ice

The place is full of Venus Fire Traps that can easily destroy you if you're not quick enough. In addition, giant ice blocks will fall from above when the Venus Fire Traps touch them, and have the ability to smush you to smithereens.

When you start this level, make a beeline for the top. Use a suit to help you get there if you have one.

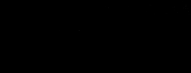

WORLD 3: SPARKLING WATERS

This beautiful, lush world is the aptly named Sparkling Waters. This area features bubbling water spouts and is south of the Layer Cake Desert endpoint; it lies east of Acorn Plains. There are nine levels here—five normal levels plus a boss fight level with Larry Koopa (who may not seem like much, but he's definitely no pushover).

1: WATERSPOUT BEACH

The geysers gush randomly. While you're waiting for this to occur, watch out for the rocks that these pesky Hickit Crabs throw or they can bleed you of health.

As you make your way through this level, keep in mind that it's not possible to enter the pipe that takes you to where the Cheep Cheeps live. You need to find another way. As you explore, you may find there is a 1-up protected by Clampy—way down at the bottom of the beach.

2: TROPICAL REFRESHER

What's the deal with all those golden pipes? Well, really no big deal as they're mainly inanimate obstacles. All you have to do is push on them to collect coins or operate other mechanisms.

Meanwhile, be prepared to roast Giant Urchins with the Fire Flower, and proceed with confidence knowing that Cheep Cheeps and Bloopers will be no match for you.

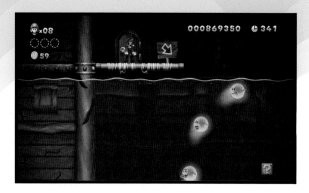

Fortress: Giant Skewer Tower

The enemies you face in this fortress include Dry Bones, Big Dry Bones, and Skewers. There is an endless stream of them so be careful not to get surrounded.

Those giant Skewers mean business. They are hard to escape from and can accumulate quickly so keep your eye out for them and try to maintain a safe distance.

Boom Boom is the end boss and is eager to try out his new moves. He'll start with a hop, then an air-spinning attack that can deal serious damage. His final attacks are two more hops and a spin, so time your dodge and countermeasures accordingly.

Ghost House: Haunted Shipwreck

There is a hidden exit that will take you through Sparkling Waters-Leaf: Skyward Stalk.

There will be obstacles. If they are close enough, they will move toward your current location, then move in a straight line and crash down on you!

Some of the doors in this Land are fake, and they turn into coins when you try to go through them.

3: ABOVE THE CHEEP CHEEP SEAS

Yoshi is an early unlock for you at this level, and you should do this first.

You can use the geysers to reach higher ground, but you have to navigate through them quickly before they recede—especially the big ones. Try to reach the exit and avoid the school of Cheep Cheeps.

If you can't, use Fireballs or Raccoon Mario's tail to dispatch them quickly and easily. Another way you can defeat them is by freezing them with an ice ball, which locks their bodies into suspended animation.

4: URCHIN SHOALS

You're going to face a variety of enemies in this game, from small and big urchins up through Koopa Troopa troops or Goombas.

Those pesky urchins though, they come at you in all different sizes, but you can defeat them all by scorching them with fireballs or freezing them with Ice Mario's ice attacks.

The giant urchin population peaks at this level, so best practice is to stay on higher ground to avoid their attacks as much as you can.

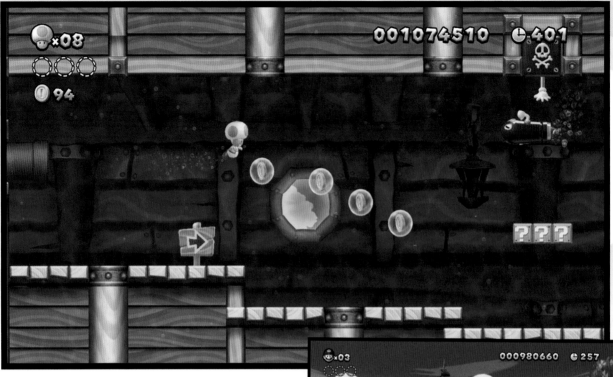

5: DRAGONEEL'S UNDERSEA GROTTO

Watch out for that nasty Dragoneel. It will be following you throughout the level. Main thing to remember here is that it can't make sharp turns, and you can always slow its roll with a volley of fireballs.

Take careful aim, as hitting its head with a fireball will slow it down, but plunking his body will actually speed him up. Be precise in your toss and timing or your handy fireballs could end up burning nobody but you in the end.

While it can be tempting to merely swim behind these creatures and remain out-of-reach while you try to take them out, don't do it for long. They'll circle back behind you, which makes you the prey, and makes hitting them even harder.

Castle: Larry's Torpedo Castle

Use an Ice Flower to kill the Dry Bones while dodging burners. Remember also to avoid the water because you can't stomp these underwater enemies.

The boss here is Larry Koopa. You fight him atop randomly spouting geysers. If you're able to stomp him three times, you will emerge the victor in battle.

Every time Larry Koopa gets hit, he goes into panic mode and tucks into his shell. He'll spin to and fro while getting a boost from the geysers that spurt sporadically on screen. When you see him finish recovering from your last hit, don't just stand there—stomp him some more!

Leaf: Skyward Stalk

Completing this level will allow you to visit Rock Candy Mines early. The key to remember here is that you don't want to fall with your leaves, so get off of them when they turn brown before it's too late.

As you make your way up the stalk, be sure to avoid the Waddlewings and Goombas flying on balloons. And don't forget to grab those Star Coins with the Flying Squirrel Suit along your climb!

Frosted Glacier is the snow-themed fourth world in this game, with pine trees and indigo mountains that are similar to World 5 from New Super Mario Bros. It features nine levels, with five of them being regular levels, two tower levels, one ghost house level, and one secret level.

This world also features Bubble Baby Yoshis, who return for the first time since their debut on the Wii U console. The boss of this world is Wendy O Koopa, who resides in Morton's Compactor Castle (Morton's Lava-Block Castle in New Super Luigi U).

1: SPINNING STAR SKY

Be careful when stepping on the star, as your weight will cause it to shift. Take an extra moment to time your jump carefully, and stay a step ahead of the indestructible Munchers on this level!

2: COOLIGAN FIELDS

In the frozen tundra of this level, Mario must navigate the Cooligan Fields and dodge and defeat the creature that bear its namesake as the main enemies.

To dispatch them, Mario must hit them once to knock off their glasses, and then he must hit them again to kill them.

Beware of various obstacles in the levels such as Warp Pipes that spawn Cooligans and lethal blocks of ice that swing up and down and can even house crowds of Cooligans.

Frosted Glacier-Fortress: Freezing Rain Tower

Mario and friends must ascend an icy tower using icicles as escalator platforms while avoiding hazards such as falling ice. The level features slippery slopes with icicles threatening from above and a section with more huge icicles that can be skipped across to reach higher platforms.

The checkpoint flag is found before the boss door, which is located at the top of the level. Here you will find two huge icicles on either side of the door, with hidden blocks above them that contain a Fire Flower and a 1-Up Mushroom.

The fourth Boom Boom is the boss of this tower, and he has been given the ability to jump by Kamek. The player must stomp on him three times before he is defeated, all while dodging icicles that are raining down from the ceiling.

3: PRICKLY GOOMBAS

One of the new power-ups in this level is the Blue Yoshi. This Yoshi has the neat ability to blow bubbles that turn enemies into coins when they are captured.

In the Frosted Glacier world, the player encounters Prickly Goombas. These enemies are similar to regular Goombas but they are covered in spikes that can damage Mario if he touches them. The best way to dispatch Prickly Goombas is to, you guessed it, not touch them! Use a fire-based attack.

4: SCALING THE MOUNTAINSIDE

In this level, you'll need to use a Super Acorn to fly to a ledge with coins and a "?" Block with a 1-Up Mushroom. Be careful of the scales—they can be lowered to reach the next platform, but they can also drop you into a pit. There are also Banzai Bills fired from a Banzai Bill Cannon, so watch out or you'll get clobbered!

5: ICICLE CAVERNS

The level features a frozen underground cavern where Mario and friends must navigate a treacherous cave of icicles, as well as bypass plenty of Buzzy Beetles.

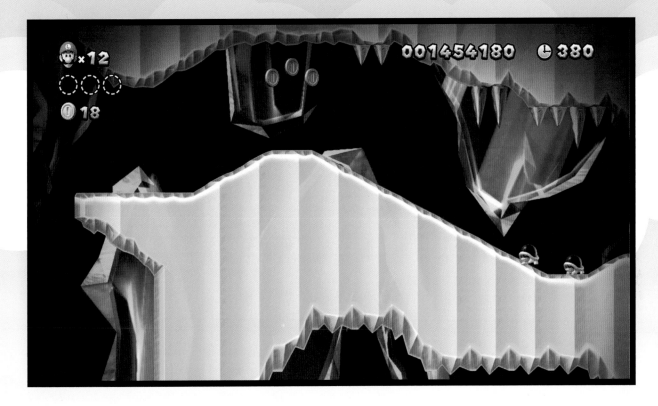

At the start of the level, you can find a hidden platform above your spawn point. Once you dodge the giant icicle falling your way, you can reach this platform by using a P-Acorn or a Balloon Baby Yoshi to fly or float to it. If you continue heading to the right, you will find the platform with the third Star Coin. You'll know you've reached the end of this level when you arrive at the Goal Pole.

Ghost House: Swinging Ghost House

This level is set in a Ghost House where the rooms and objects all swing back and forth slowly, which can really mess with your timing.

You start off next to a wall of brick blocks that block a Warp Door which you must enter. Once you do, the screen scrolls left, and you'll find a Boo, a "?" Block containing a power-up, and a P-Switch. The P-Switch causes blue coins to appear and turns the brick blocks into coins!

Also in the Ghost House, a secret portal: can you find the disguised exit leading to **Frosted Glacier-Fliprus: Fliprus Lake?**

Castle: Wendys Shifting Castle

The main challenge in this part of the level comes from negotiating the shifting girders, which can be tricky to keep track of, while avoiding the various Thwomps and Dry Bones scattered throughout. Winning the boss battle versus Wendy O. Koopa is not easy, as she can easily pummel you with shards of icy spikes if you're not quick afoot.

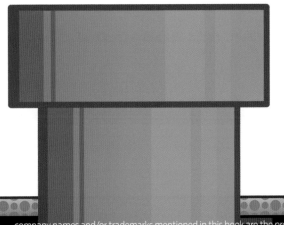

Frosted Glacier: Fliprus Lake

This is where you'll encounter the Flipruses. These creatures are essentially Walruses that hurl avalanche snowballs at you. But don't take their odd cuteness for weakness, as their snowballs can deal enough damage to kill you. Stomp on the incoming snowballs to squash them, or use any other offensive means you have in your current inventory to dispatch them.

As in most levels, there are also River Piranha Plants. They blow spike green balls in the air similar to the Ptooies from Super Mario Bros. 3. If you're able to overcome their attack, Piranha Plants will panic in a sweat as they are otherwise powerless.

WORLD 5: SODA JUNGLE

The largest world in the game, Soda Jungle is a lush, jungle-themed series of courses based on Giant Land from Super Mario Bros. 3 and Forest of Illusion from Super Mario World.

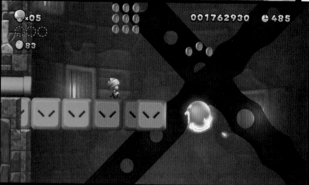

Stocked full of colossal enemies and obstacles, it is also home to Iggy Koopa, the fifth boss in the game. The world contains 12 levels, including five normal levels, two enemy courses, an airship level, a tower level, and a castle level. There are also three Toad Houses in the Soda Jungle.

Soda Jungle-Airship: The Mighty Cannonship

The first airship to appear which also marks the kickoff to Soda Jungle, this level opens near a Mechakoopa, firing cannons, and a "?" Block containing a power-up.

Dodge the three firing guns and find the red warp pipe that leads to Bowser Jr. and his Clown Car, which is in submarine mode. He'll fire Targeting Teds at you that you must redirect to sink his submersible. It takes three hits to take him out and drain the chamber, allowing you to venture forth into Soda Jungle.

1: JUNGLE OF THE GIANTS

Jungle of the Giants takes place in a world filled with oversized enemies and ominous obstacles. This level also features a series of large structures, some of which are made up of Mega Blocks. Bigger versions of familiar foes include:

- Big Goombas
- Big Koopa Troopas
- Big Piranha Plants

2: BRIDGE OVER POISONED WATERS

1. Use a Super Acorn to get to the Star Coin at the start of the level.

2. Don't stay still on the logs for too long, or they will roll you into the poison water.

3. A secret exit leading to Soda Jungle-6: Seesaw Bridge is on this level. Keep looking until you find it!

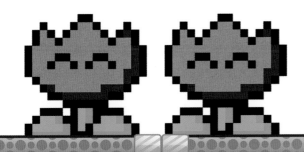

3: BRAMBALL WOODS

The overall vibe of Bramball Woods is dark and foggy, and it features Bramballs as enemies, the only level in the game where you will find them. They move forward awkwardly in a slinky-like motion, but touching their feet or arms causes damage. Take them out by leaping and landing on the ball at their center mass, or use one of your various offensive range attacks.

Fortress: Snake Block Tower

Without careful timing and jumps, the Snake Block Tower is a difficult level to complete. You may need to practice this one a few times before you succeed, so don't become discouraged.

1. Stay on the snake block and jump past the Amps, Big Amps, and swinging chain balls.

2. Stomp on Boom Boom's head to stun him, and hit him three times to defeat him.

Ghost House: Which-Way Labyrinth

In this spooky scene, you will spot a brick with a glowing Baby Yoshi. Use the light emitted by the Glowing Baby Yoshi to confuse the Scaredy Rats and make them run in the opposite direction.

You can also find a secret exit leading to Soda Jungle-ParaBeetle on this level. Where might it be in a ghost house?

4: PAINTED SWAMPLAND

There are a few things you must be extremely cautious about in this level:

1. The first is the water—it's filled with poison, so stay out of it!

2. Warp Pipes—random ones will sink when you step on them, so move nimbly.

3. Boos—there are quite a few of them, so watch out!

PRO TIP: Be sure to collect all the red rings on this level, as they will lead you to a secret exit to Soda Jungle-6: Seesaw Bridge!

5: DEEPSEA RUINS

Be careful of the Jellybeams in the water but take advantage of their unique qualities—they light up the area as you swim, but they can still hurt you if they touch you.

6: SEESAW BRIDGE

When you start the level, make your way over to the three "?" Blocks and hit the one that contains a power-up. You can always use another one, and it will give you a pivotal edge later in the level.

Next, make your way across the Seesaw Bridges. Take a moment to get your timing down before you try to rush through their constant tilting up on down.

7: WIGGLER STAMPEDE

Plan to harness the power of Big Wigglers to get past the poison and reach the Goal Pole. Top tips for completing this level include:

· Use a Big Wiggler to cross the poison and reach the checkpoint flag safely.

· Turn the Big Wiggler into a trampoline! Use it to jump and reach the coins and hit the next P-Switch.

Soda Jungle - Castle: Iggy's Volcanic Castle

The main thing to remember here is that the lava is hot, and kills quickly! As such:

· Make use of the moving platforms to ride above the lava safely.

· Try to stay on higher ground as this will allow you to avoid the "waves" of lava.

· Use your Super Leaf when you can to fly over lava pits.

ParaBeetle: Flight of the Para-Beetles

A few pointers to keep in mind when navigating this beetle bonanza:

· Use the Para-Beetles to reach the "?" bricks that contain power-ups and grab those first.

· Be deft when dealing with the Heavy Para-Beetles as they can smash you quickly.

· Enter the Warp Pipes at the top of the level to reach the Goal Pole.

WORLD 6: ROCK-CANDY MINES

The sixth world of New Super Mario Bros. U Deluxe is the mountainous Rock-Candy Mines. It's a small world with only 10 levels and lies east of Acorn Plains. Train tracks act as bridges across gaps in this world, creating unique circumstances in this world.

1: FUZZY CLIFFTOP

You can use Yoshi to eat the Fuzzies, but beware of the two Ice Piranha Plants on this level. The first Ice Piranha Plant appears near the beginning while the second shows up at the end. Between the two, take care to collect all the berries that you can find on the bushes along the way.

2: PORCUPUFFER FALLS

The best tip for this level is to make sure you stay underwater as much as possible. It will keep you safe from the Porcupuffer. If you're able to elude him you should be able to reach the Checkpoint Flag at the end of the falls, but watch out for the Paratroopas who pop-up!

Tower: Grinding-Stone Tower

Here's best practices for navigating this level:

1. Use the Warp Pipes to transport yourself more quickly.

2. Keep in mind that some of the Bony Beetles have spikes.

3. Be on the lookout for the Grrrols that spawn throughout the level.

4. Don't forget to collect the coins and Mini Mushroom.

5. There is a secret exit on this level leading to Rock Candy Mines: Thrilling Spine Coaster.

3: WADDLEWING'S NEST

This level can be a bit tricky, but the best way to get through it is to use the Chain Chomps to your advantage. There are a few spots where you can break the bricks with them so find those spots and proceed accordingly.

You'll also want to watch out for the tilting platforms, as slipping off them is painfully easy.

4: LIGHT BLOCKS, DARK TOWER

You'll need to persevere through a dank cave lit only by occasional blocks of light. To get through, you should:

· Use invincibility if you need to make a quick escape; grabbing and using the star available at the beginning of the level will keep you safe from the get-go.

· Pay close attention to the light blocks, they can help guide you through the darkness.

5: WALKING PIRANHA PLANTS!

What's worse than Piranha Plants? Stalking Piranha Plants on lifts that move! Use a Koopa shell to knock out many at once, or use an Ice Flower to freeze them to death.

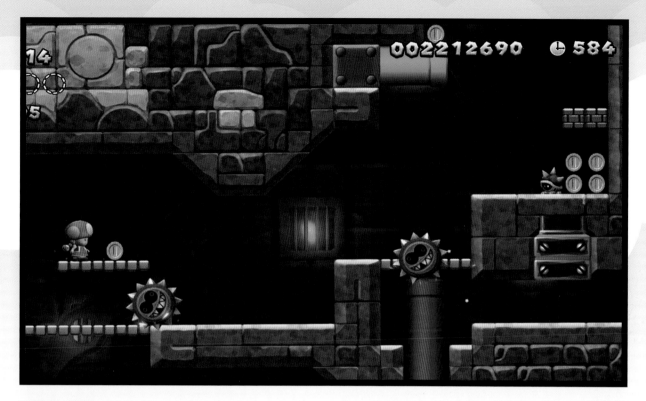

PRO TIP: Keep your eyes peeled for the secret exit on this level.

6: THRILLING SPINE COASTER

Here's what to know for this level:

1. Make sure to hit the "?" switch to create blocks under the coins.

2. Be on the lookout for the Super Star power-up, as it will help you take out any enemies you encounter.

3. Beware that the coaster dips into the poisoned water!

Tower: Screwtop Tower

Look out for Bony Beetles and Sumo Bros, and be careful when traversing the platforms as there are L-shaped Fire Bars.

The Checkpoint Flag is located shortly after you make it past the Fire Bars, so be sure to save your game in case you need to restart

from this point. To defeat the Boss Sumo Bro, hit him hard from below when he's standing on one of the platforms and then stomp him.

7: SHIFTING-FLOOR CAVE

The Spike Tops can be lethal if they corner you; the Swoops can be a nuisance; and watch out for the Big Piranha Plants at the end of the level. Use your power-ups wisely to take out as many enemies as possible in one use.

Castle: Roy's Conveyor Castle

To get through this castle, bear in mind the following:

· There are blocks containing a 1-Up Mushroom early in the level and near the end.

· Dry Bones and Bony Beetles are your enemies.

· Iron blocks fall from conveyor belts—which you can recycle as platforms.

· Lava bubbles can jump out of lava pits.

· The boss door leads to an area with a cannon which launches you to Roy Koopa.

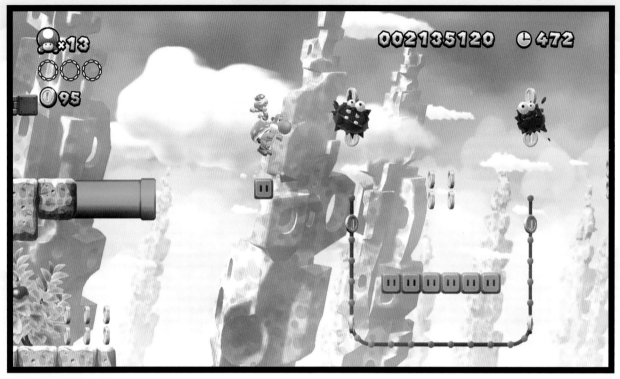

WORLD 7: MERINGUE CLOUDS

World 7 is cloudy and lies east of Acorn Plains and south of Peach's Castle. The world is accessed by completing Roy's Conveyor Castle or completing Flight of the Para-Beetles. It is a sky world similar to World 7 from previous New Super Mario games, but unlike those, Meringue Clouds takes place at dusk.

1: LAND OF FLYING BLOCKS

To get through the first level, you should:

1. Make sure to use the cloud platform to navigate the area.

2. Be ready to snatch the coins in bubbles and blocks that appear when you reach certain spots.

3. Lookout for the Piranha Plants lurking in Warp Pipes.

4. Make use of the Trampoline in a "?" Block.

2: SEESAW SHROOMS

Use a fire flower to take care of the Fuzzy. You'll also encounter some Seesaw Shrooms, which can be tricky to navigate so use Yoshi's egg to do hover jumps. There are also some Lakitus in the level, so be sure to steer clear of their spiky eggs.

3: SWITCHBACK HILL

Top tips for Switchback Hill include:

· Use the arrow lifts to your advantage, and avoid the Bullet Bills by ducking underneath them.

· In some areas, you'll have to duck under walls.

· You'll uncover an Ice Flower power-up after reaching the checkpoint.

· Jump across the switchbacks to get to the other side.

Tower: Slide Lift Tower

Progress through the level by using the Slide Lifts. There are Fire Bros and Dry Bones in this level, so be careful. The Super Star is in a "?" Block, so get it if you need it. There are also Warp Pipes in the level.

The Magikoopa is the sub-boss that will launch magic beams at you. When he fires the platforms, scamper on them to get a better angle of attack against him and stomp on him three times when you can to defeat him.

Ghost House: Spinning Spirit House

Some things you need to watch out for:

1. Pay attention to the moving platform; be patient and time your jumps correctly.

2. Be careful of the Big Boos. They can be hard to avoid, especially if you're trying to hurry through the level, but they won't be ignored.

PRO TIP: There is a secret exit that leads to Meringue Clouds-Castle: Ludwig's Clockwork Tower.

4: BOUNCY CLOUD BOOMERANGS

· Make use of the Bouncy Clouds to help navigate your way past the Goombas and Piranha Plants.

· Make sure you grab the Ice Flower; you may not need it immediately but it will come in handy later on in the level.

· Be careful of the Boomerang Bros scattered about the level—they can easily end your game if you're not paying attention.

5: A QUICK DIP IN THE SKY

On this level, you will find Water Balls that can help you progress vertically, and also use the paratrooper to fly to the top of the flagpole. The first power-up you see is the Fire Flower, which will come in quite handy against the Piranha Plants.

6: SNAKING ABOVE MIST VALLEY

You must stay on a snake platform as the level scrolls. Falling off results in game over, so keep in mind the following:

· The Flying Squirrel suit can help you stay aloft.

· Take care to avoid the Fire Brother's lethal fireballs.

Castle: Ludwig's Clockwork Castle

To survive this level, you should be aware of the moving platforms that can crush you, while taking advantage of all the various "?" Blocks that are made available. You should also be on the lookout for Bony Beetles and Sledge Bros, who are all too happy to end your game.

Airship: Boarding the Airship

The level features a Remote-Control Platform that you must use to progress further. The final section is a boss battle against Bowser Jr. in his trusty Junior Clown Car. He will destroy the

steel blocks you're using, so be prepared to hit him with everything in your arsenal.

You can harm him by using Bob-ombs that he throws at you, and vanquish him after three hits.

WORLD 8: PEACH'S CASTLE

The final world in this game is Peach's Castle. After Bowser and his Koopalings have kidnapped Princess Peach, they raid the castle and claim it as their own. Then Kamek's tornado comes along. Six levels make up this world with no Toad House or Enemy Course.

PRO TIP: At the end of this level (and game) you can see a restored version of Peach's Castle, but if you play the post-endgame, you'll find out what happened during the tornado.

1: METEOR MOAT

Players must navigate a treacherous level filled with raining debris and lava geysers. Make sure to pay close attention to the movement of the platforms and ground, and avoid standing on any of them that are about to sink into the lava.

PRO TIP: A secret exit leads to Peach's Castle-4: Firefall Cliffs.

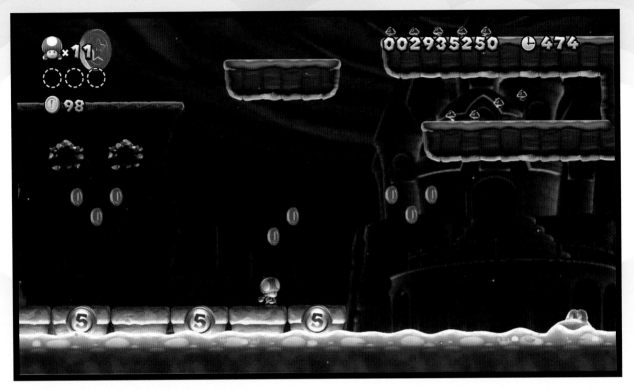

2: MAGMA-RIVER CRUISE

Key survival tips for this level include:

1. Watch out for the Magmaws—these creatures cannot be defeated and will cause instant death if they touch you.

2. Pay attention to the number of enemies on the Limited Lift—if this reaches 0, the ride will end prematurely.

3. Be sure to collect the Ice Flower power-up located in a "?" block midway through the level. It will allow you to freeze enemies, making them easier to defeat.

3: RISING TIDES OF LAVA

In this level, you should:

· Plan to walk on Big Buzzy Beetles as platforms to safely cross over lava. They are lava-immune, so you can stand on their shells without taking damage.

· Pay close attention to the screw tops and how they work. You'll need to use them to help you progress through the level.

4: FIREFALL CLIFFS

As the game nears its climax, it's more important than ever to keep some important tips in mind:

1. Stay aware of your surroundings. This includes watching out for meteors that fall from above and avoiding pits of lava that bubble up from below.

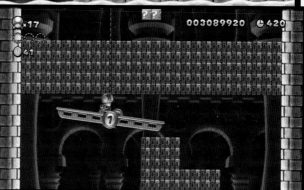

2. Be nimble and quick. This means never stay in one place too long, and don't be afraid to try climbing up walls or jumping over pits.

3. Use your resources wisely. For example, destroy Hard Blocks with Meteors and always try to amass as many helpful items, like Super Stars and 1-Up Mushrooms, as possible.

Castle: Red-Hot Elevator Ride

The rising lava will overtake you if you're not mindful, so be conscious that it's constantly flowing in. Also keep in mind that when an enemy lands on the elevator it stops moving, so be patient and plan for delays without panic, as you try to ride out the elevator to the end of the level.

Castle: The Final Battle

In this level, you must face off against Bowser and Bowser Jr. to save Princess Peach. Tips for defeating them include:

- Pepper Bowser with fireballs whenever you can. It will bleed out his health and make the battle go more quickly.

- Be careful when Bowser does ground stomps, as it causes the entire platform to sink into the lava!

- Don't get greedy on offense, always be ready to dodge Bowser's fireballs and spinning shell, as well as Bowser Jr.'s diving attacks and dropped Bob-ombs.

If you've taken our advice to heart then kudos are in order, as you should have reached the end of the game. Congratulations!

TIPS FROM THE CLUBHOUSE FOR MARIO GOLF: SUPER RUSH

Let's get one thing clear from the get-go, Mario Golf: Super Rush on Nintendo Switch is the latest and greatest Mario golf game, and while it has all the elements we've all come to know and love about this iconic series in the Mario pantheon of games, the speed element makes it an entirely different animal.

You can play traditional matches against friends or NPCs, or you can play in Rush mode, where you are racing against up to three other players to finish the hole first.

Here are some tips from our club pro:

TALKIN' ABOUT PRACTICE

Since you're basically playing a round of golf in hurry-up fashion in Rush mode, the best thing you can do is practice, practice, practice your shots, spins, handling wind effect, and more, on your own. That way, when you go up against friends and family, your decisions and strokes will be second nature as you hit fairways and greens while they struggle to finish holes.

FOCUS ON PUTTING

Even Tiger Woods and Bryson DeChambeau know that matches are won and lost on the putting green, and there's no shortcut to reading greens and breaks. On your putting grid, blue means the green has a gradual break in the direction the arrow is pointing, while red means it's steep. The game provides plenty of data for your stroke, but you should also review your putt from above to see if you have a little or a lot of space to the left, right or behind the hole.

STUDY THE SPECIAL SHOTS

Each character has a special shot, and you should try them all out so you are familiar with what effects they have on a round. Wario's shot, for example, gives him the ability to drop a lightning cloud on the course, which is nice to know before you get zapped during a good round. You want to know these shots like the back of your hand when you play in Story Mode, where speed golf is required.

DASH FOR HEART HEALTH

When dashing in speed golf rounds, try to sprint from one heart power-up to the next. They refill your stamina and if you get your timing and directions right, you can sprint from heart to heart all the way to the pin while keeping your stamina close to max.

KNOW A BAD LIE WHEN YOU SEE ONE

When you find your ball on an up or down slope or in the brush, your lie will be displayed in the shot meter. The meter will indicate which way the ball will fly after you strike it, so compensate for the curve accordingly. In deep grass you can count on losing some distance just to get your ball aloft, so muscle up and let 'er rip.

PUT A SPIN ON THINGS

Learning how far you can hit a shot with each character is useful, and once you learn this info you can play through the game, but real pros know that using spin is what separates the wannabes from the winners. You must learn to use topspin and backspin on your shots to hit more efficiently and save strokes on your scorecard. As you advance you gain ever more control of your spin shots so it is better to start learning and using spin control from the get-go.

BE THE BALL

As the legendary Carl the groundskeeper in *Caddyshack* said, "be the ball." What we mean by this is that you should play within yourself for the most part, and only go for broke when you have to. It's much better to be on the fairway 250 yards off the tee than in the rough or among trees 280 yards from the tee. This golf truism is especially applicable in Golf Adventure mode, where it can be tempting to hit as far as you can to get out front. Rushing too much usually drops you behind, so stay on the fairways and layup when it's there, instead of blasting for the greens.

SUPER MARIO 3D WORLD + BOWSER'S FURY

Super Mario 3D World + Bowser's Fury is a sprawling world of all the things we've come to know and love about Mario and his rich tapestry of games.

In it, Green Stars are the most common item you collect. You don't need to find them all to complete the game, but you need them to unlock all the optional areas.

That said, the Green Stars are literally sprinkled throughout the levels and they certainly help encourage the exploring process, so we suggest using them as sort of reverse breadcrumbs—scour every square inch of each environment you're in and try to collect the nearly 400 that are available. How many can you find?

By practicing this technique, you're basically hoisting yourself through the game and its many levels.

Meanwhile, we're going to focus this guide on the two meatiest parts of this Mario title: collecting Stamps and the Bowser's Fury game story.

COLLECTING STAMPS

You earn a Stamp for every level that you complete, and there are more than 80 Stamps to collect. With all that work to do, let's drill down and get our collection started.

WORLD 1-1: SUPER BELL HILL

Go through the green pipe to the left of the tall bell tree. Once you're in, enter the clear pipe and come out on top and you'll find the Stamp.

WORLD 1-2: KOOPA TROOPA CAVE

To reach the Stamp, go through the pipe to the area with a single long block. If you jump on it, you'll reveal another hidden block. Keep repeating this move. You'll soon reach the top of the ledge and are able to enter the clear pipe on the wall that takes you to the room with the Stamp.

WORLD 1-3: MOUNT BEANPOLE

The Stamp is wedged in a tight spot. Try to get to higher ground and you can simply walk over the edge to fall on it and claim it as your own.

WORLD 1-4: PLESSIE'S PLUNGING FALLS

The Stamp is easy to see on the bend of the river, but taking the correct angle to snag it without falling off the edge is not. Time your turn and swing into it at the right moment.

WORLD 1-5: SWITCH SCRAMBLE CIRCUS

Flip over all the tiles in front of the flagpole to yellow and a platform with a Stamp on it will drop down.

WORLD 1-CASTLE: BOWSER'S HIGHWAY SHOWDOWN

Use the soccer balls to smash the four big brick blocks to snatch your Stamp.

WORLD 2-1: CONKDOR CANYON

Easy; it's sitting in front of the path that leads to the flagpole.

WORLD 2-2: PUFFPROD PEAKS

Lift the platforms under the blocks at the beginning of the level. One will reveal a chute you can drop through to grab your Stamp.

WORLD 2-3: SHADOW-PLAY ALLEY

Just before reaching the menacing Piranha Plant in the shadowy alley, drop into the lower chamber and smash the crates to claim your Stamp.

WORLD 2-4: REALLY ROLLING HILLS

You must use Mario to complete this task. Roll rightward over the hills towards the pond. Flip the Mario switch and get yer Stamp.

WORLD 2-5: DOUBLE CHERRY PASS

Three "?" blocks lie to the right of the red ring. Use a Double Cherry, and have one of your duplicates stand on the left block, and another smack it from below. The block will escalate and reveal your Stamp.

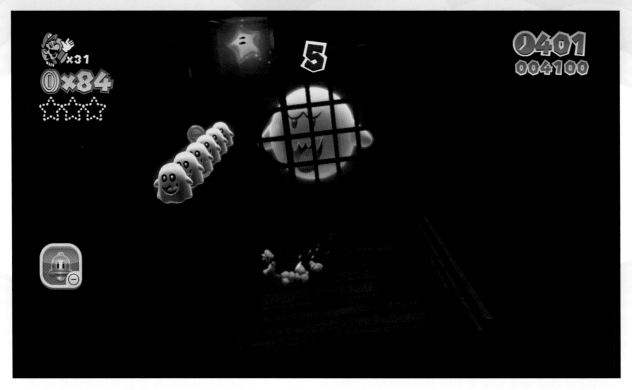

WORLD 2-CASTLE: BOWSER'S BULLET BILL BRIGADE

When you reach the part with a metal grate, sprint to the front of it and try and leap up and latch onto the Stamp before the window closes.

WORLD 2-TENT

It's nice to have an easy one at the end of a world. Watch the world map for a tent to pop-up. When it does, simply go inside for your final Stamp from World 2.

WORLD 3-1: SNOWBALL PARK

The Stamp is perched precariously on the far lip of a slippery, icy pit. Skirt the edge slowly to score your Stamp!

WORLD 3-2: CHAIN-LINK CHARGE

It's best to be in Cat form for this level, as you can easily crawl your way up the chain-link fence and secure your Stamp.

WORLD 3-3: SHIFTY BOO MANSION

When there are ghosts around, it makes sense that floating might be part of your answer to your Stamp seeking. Plop on the love seat at the start of the level and it'll spirit you away to the Stamp above.

WORLD 3-4: PRETTY PLAZA PANIC

A Peach switch lies to the left of the spinning platforms. You must be playing as Peach to claim your Stamp.

WORLD 3-5: PIPELINE LAGOON

The Stamp is tucked in a secret chamber you must swim into before reaching the sunken ship.

WORLD 3-6: MOUNT MUST DASH

Catapult yourself to the top of the level by bouncing off the jump panels and mushrooms. The Stamp sits at the highest point.

WORLD 3-7: SWITCHBOARD FALLS

Jump on the lift and ride it all the way to the left. When it pauses, leap to the next lift and it will whisk you away to your next Stamp.

WORLD 3-TRAIN: THE BULLET BILL EXPRESS

You will find the Stamp on the ledge below Pom Pom. The catch is, a Fire Bro is guarding it.

WORLD 4-1: ANT TROOPER HILL

You will find it protected by pesky ants in the first cave you can enter. Send the ants marching to their death before snatching your Stamp.

WORLD 4-2: PIRANHA CREEPER CREEK

The right side is the theme of this level. Before entering the water, boost off the Piranha Plant on the right to enter the nearby hole. Once you're through, keep running right until you reach the Stamp.

WORLD 4-3: BEEP BLOCK SKYWAY

Behind the Checkpoint flag is an elevator that requires three characters to activate. Break out a Double Cherry and ride together to the Stamp above.

WORLD 4-4: BIG BOUNCE BYWAY

The Stamp floats among a large flock of Para-Biddybuds. Bounce off the giant mushroom to spring to your prize.

WORLD 4-5: SPIKE'S LOST CITY

Activate a Super Bell and climb the wall to the left of the green warp pipe. Keep walking to the left until you happen upon the Buddy-buddy Stamp.

WORLD 4-CASTLE: LAVA ROCK LAIR

Activate a Super Bell and crawl up the left wall in Cat form, where you will find the Stamp sitting at the top.

WORLD 4-TENT

Another easy tent level! Simply enter the tent and claim your latest Stamp, no muss, no fuss.

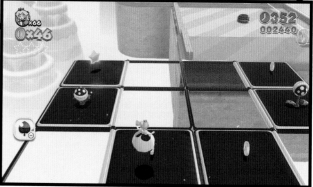

WORLD 5-1: SUNSHINE SEASIDE
While riding Plessie, keep right and be ready to disembark on the three small platforms. You will find the Stamp on the third platform.

WORLD 5-2: TRICKY TRAPEZE THEATER
Once you're able to elevate over and escape the Piranha Plants below, head left to find the Stamp.

WORLD 5-3: BACKSTREET BUSTLE
A Toad switch sits on the right side of the room. Toad is the only one who can reveal this Stamp.

WORLD 5-4: SPRAWLING SAVANNAH
Follow the column of ants marching through a large field into their hole to reveal a Queen ant carrying the Stamp on its back.

WORLD 5-5: BOB-OMBS BELOW
Once you're able to clear the circular platform with the rabbit, use a Bob-omb to blast open the crack in the wall. Enter the opening and run right to get your Stamp.

WORLD 5-6: CAKEWALK FLIP
Bring two characters to the end of the level using a Double Cherry. Once there, jump on the elevator together and it'll take you to the Stamp.

WORLD 5-7: SEARCHLIGHT SNEAK
While you can see this Stamp tucked above a row of blocks, you have to stay out of the spotlight as you attempt to jump up and reach it.

WORLD 5-CASTLE: KING KA-THUNK'S CASTLE
Yet another spot where you need a Super Bell, climb the area above the Chargin' Chucks in Cat form to reach your latest Stamp.

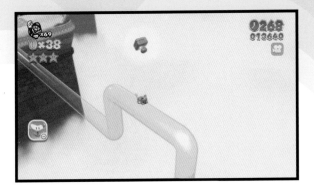

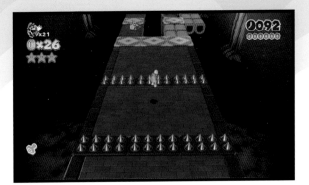

WORLD 5-TENT

Yay! Another tent and another easy-to-get Stamp.

WORLD 6-1: CLEAR PIPE CRUISE

Just after the second Green Star, you'll see a long clear pipe. Hop onto it, not into it, and run until you find the Stamp floating above.

WORLD 6-2: SPOOKY SEASICK WRECK

For this Stamp, you can try and slip past a ring of Peepas guarding it, or burn the Super Star on the right side of the room and plow through them.

WORLD 6-3: HANDS-ON HALL

Enter the warp pipe, but be sure you have a Propeller Block. When you reach the spikes, follow the rollers to discover a portal to the outside. Use the Propeller to ascend to the roof where you'll find your next Stamp.

WORLD 6-4: DEEP JUNGLE DRIFT

The moving grates will eventually shuffle you to the Stamp at the end of the level, so step lively!

WORLD 6-5: TY-FOO FLURRIES

When you first hit the ice, use a Goomba's Shoe to ride to the spikes on the right, and you will find the Stamp sitting there.

WORLD 6-6: BULLET BILL BASE

Go to the left of the flagpole and you will find a row of blocks with a Stamp suspended above.

WORLD 6-7: FUZZY TIME MINE

About halfway through the level in a small section of the wall, you'll find this Stamp. Just wait for the platforms to clear out and claim it when you can.

WORLD 6-CASTLE: BOWSER'S BOB-OMB BRIGADE

Use a bomb to destroy the brick block sitting on the right path just after the fork in the road, and you'll find the Stamp hidden inside.

WORLD 6-TENT

Waltz into the tent for another free Stamp.

WORLD CASTLE-1: FORT FIRE BROS.

When you see the Firebar with a "?" Block before the Goomba Tower, ground pound the block and it'll elevate and guide you to the Stamp.

WORLD CASTLE-2: SWITCHBLACK RUINS

Jump to the right of the moving platform to find a secret chamber that houses the Stamp.

WORLD CASTLE-3:

Stay to the left of the donut lifts, and then jump across the gap when you can to grab your next Stamp.

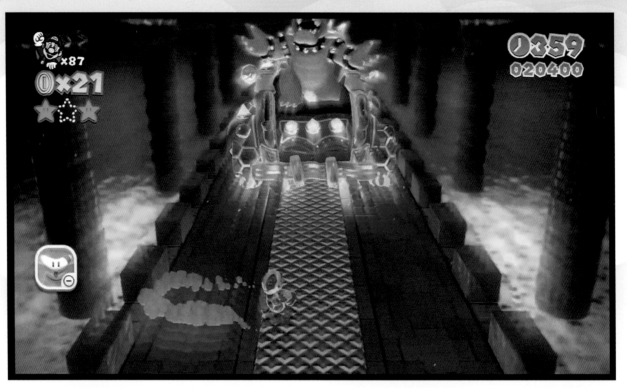

WORLD CASTLE-4: BOILING BLUE BULLY BELL

You will notice a small ledge to the left of the platforms with the arrows. Jump off the platform and onto the ledge for your next Stamp.

WORLD CASTLE-5: TRICK TRAP TOWER

After finding the first Green Star, use a Super Bell and climb the wall to claim your Stamp floating on the clouds.

WORLD CASTLE-6: RAMMERHEAD REEF

You will see a small cubby in the wall at the end of the level. If you can dodge the Rammerheads you will find the Stamp nestled inside.

WORLD CASTLE-7: SIMMERING LAVA LAKE

While you can see this Stamp under a grate where lava flows, you have to get your timing down first. Pop-in and pop-out with the Stamp before the lava burns you.

WORLD CASTLE-CASTLE: BOWSER'S LAVA LAKE KEEP

This Stamp is hidden above the switch you hit to open and close the bridge. Use wall jumps to ascend and snag your Stamp.

WORLD CASTLE-TENT

Hooray, another easy peasy tent Stamp!

WORLD BOWSER-1: SPIKY SPIKE BRIDGE

Run left towards the direction of the spikes after you reach the checkpoint flag, and you'll find the Stamp at the end.

WORLD BOWSER-2: PLESSIE'S DUNE DOWNHILL

Steer Plessie between the two giant Bowser sculptures and you'll be able to discern a path hidden in the clouds that will lead you to the Stamp.

WORLD BOWSER-3: COOKIE COGWORKS

Watch the hole where the first row of ants is marching from. Drop into it and you'll find the next Stamp tucked amongst them.

WORLD BOWSER-TRAIN: THE BOWSER EXPRESS

While you can see the Stamp on the roof of one of the carts, you have to ground pound the "?" Block on the right and it'll connect you to the roof.

WORLD BOWSER-4: FOOTLIGHT LANE

Jump to the right of the platform with a glowing center and you'll find a secret passage that takes you to the Stamp.

WORLD BOWSER-5: DEEPWATER DUNGEON

While swimming, allow the floating blobs of water, to lift you to the roof, where you'll find the Stamp above one of the large spiky obstacles.

WORLD BOWSER-6: A BEAM IN THE DARK

On the first moving platform you'll see a Luigi switch. You must hop on it as Luigi to activate and earn this Stamp.

WORLD BOWSER-7: GRUMBLUMP INFERNO

Ride down the twisting platform after the checkpoint flag until you see a Hammer Bro. Jump squarely on him and grab your Stamp.

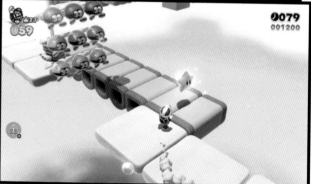

WORLD BOWSER-CASTLE: THE GREAT TOWER OF BOWSER LAND
You'll find the Stamp in the bell tree to the left of the flagpole after defeating Meowser.

WORLD BOWSER-TENT
Pop into the tent for your free Stamp!

WORLD STAR-1: RAINBOW RUN
Stay right while riding Plessie and you'll find the Stamp tucked between two gold rings.

WORLD STAR-2: SUPER GALAXY
After the Checkpoint Flag, use a Super Bell and climb in cat form to the top of the area. You'll find three platforms that form a wall when flipped, which you can climb and claim the Stamp.

WORLD STAR-3: ROLLING RIDE RUN
As you roll on the spinning platform, take the path on the right and you'll see a switch that only Rosalina can activate. Flip it for your next Stamp.

WORLD STAR-4: THE GREAT GOAL POLE
While you can easily spot the Stamp behind the Walleye, getting to it is another matter.

WORLD STAR-5: SUPER BLOCK LAND
Toss a Bob-omb or smash through the giant brick block wedged in the ground in Mega form to find the Stamp hidden below.

WORLD STAR-6: HONEYCOMB STARWAY
When facing the bees near the end of the stage, you can see the Stamp on the right. You must use a boomerang to get it.

WORLD STAR-7: GARGANTUAN GROTTO

You need a Mega Mushroom to break the giant brick blocks above the sign to find the Stamp.

WORLD STAR-8: PEEPA'S FOG BOG

Follow the path on the right before the end of the foggy area, and you'll find the Stamp.

WORLD STAR-9: COSMIC CANNON CLUSTER

While you can see this Stamp early in the level, you must use a Cannon Block to destroy the "?" Blocks in front of the Stamp.

WORLD STAR-TENT

Another freebie inside. Go get it!

WORLD CROWN-TOAD: CAPTAIN TOAD'S FIERY FINALE

You have to get onto the cloud to complete the level, since that's where the Stamp is hidden.

WORLD CROWN-MYSTERY HOUSE: MYSTERY HOUSE MARATHON

If you can make it to the last level of the Mystery House, you'll find this Stamp sitting on the path.

WORLD CROWN-CROWN: CHAMPION'S ROAD

If you can reach the end of this level, you'll be rewarded with a Stamp sitting there for the taking.

WORLD CROWN-TENT

Another stroll into a tent for another easy Stamp.

FINAL 5 STAMPS

To get the last five stamps, you must beat every level with each of the five playable characters. Once you master the game with one character and are familiar with the challenges, the rest should come a little easier.

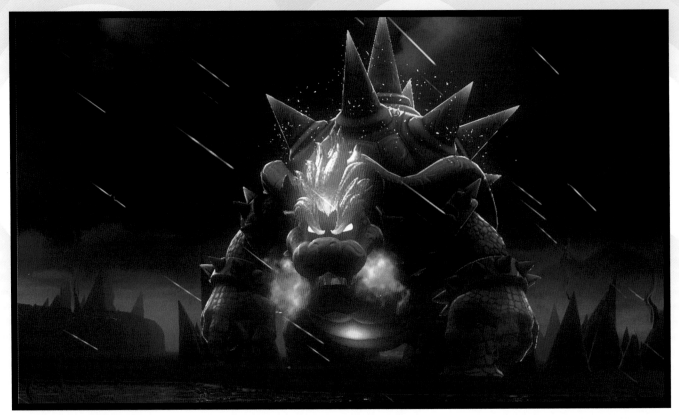

BOWSER'S FURY

In this deep side-story game, a black sludge coats Fury Bowser while he repeatedly engulfs the 3D World island in fiery attacks. Fury Spikes rain from above as Fury Bowser strikes with fireballs and beams. Your goal is to collect Cat Shines, which you use in a variety of ways to stop this onslaught.

PRO TIP: A Cat Shine can make the lighthouse brighten the immediate area and forces Fury Bowser to retreat.

At the outset, keep in mind that Giga Bells in Lake Lapcat can only be activated by collecting Cat Shines. When awakened, they conjure Giga Cat Mario to fight Fury Bowser.

If you can't stop Fury Bowser he will transform into Giant Bowser and literally give you an even bigger problem. If you must face Giant Bowser, the secret to winning is to use Mario to break the protective layer surrounding the three Giga Bells, while dodging attacks from him.

Upon defeating Giant Bowser, Bowser Jr. returns to tell Mario he must help him deal with Fury Bowser until more Cat Shines are collected. Fortunately, new Cat Shines are now marked on the map; you will have the ability to warp to previously explored islands; and Cat Plessie can now carry kittens!

PRO TIP: If you collect all 100 Cat Shines you can change your Cat Suit to resemble Giga Cat Mario, in addition to a cat form of Bowser Jr. and his Clown Car.

PLAYABLE CHARACTERS

MARIO

Mario is the only character from Super Mario 3D World playable in Bowser's Fury edition. He lacks his companions' special abilities, but no worries! Mario will often be in cat form collecting Cat Shines and using power-ups to navigate in this world.

BOWSER JR.

Bowser Jr. is controlled by AI to help Mario, but can be replaced by a second player in two-player mode. Bowser Jr. fights to save his father using his special abilities outside of power-ups. Bowser Jr. can help Mario collect Cat Shines to restore his father—you can decide how much he helps.

You can also control Bowser Jr. in single-player mode while making him go around collecting coins and Cat Shine Shards swinging his paintbrush. Certain areas of the game will highlight after Fury Bowser is activated, and Bowser Jr. can be sent there for coins.

Another cool feature of Bowser Jr. is that his Amiibo will explode when scanned, defeating enemies and shattering nearby items and blocks.

PRO TIP: 100 Cat Shines are needed to turn Bowser Jr. into a cat, and his car ends up with whiskers as well. Meow!

OTHER CHARACTERS

KITTENS

Kittens are small, adorable, populous creatures who appear in Super Mario 3D World. A colony of kittens inhabits most of the islands in Lake Lapcat, and they each have different colors.

PRO TIP: The Maneki-Neko is the lucky symbol that these kitties' different colors represent. Learn the color schemes so you know them like the back of your paw.

As you explore, you will see them frolicking, lounging, or dozing off. Kittens are known to lunge at Green Shells in an attempt to break them for a Lucky Bell.

The Kittens of Lake Lapcat are friendly and love to play with Cat Mario, but not in his other forms. If he's Cat Mario, the kittens will follow him around but otherwise, they are scared of Mario and will avoid him.

Cat Mario's new pet kitten can scratch to attack enemies when held. They can help you destroy Brick Blocks as Cat Mario does, and can also share a ride on the back of Cat Plessie after clearing the game.

Scores of kittens roam the world, inhabiting each of the following areas:

· Scamper Shores
· Fort Flaptrap
· Near a lighthouse on Pounce Bounce Island
· Near a lighthouse on Roiling Roller Island
· Mount Magmeow
· Pipe Path Tower
· Wasteland Gigabell

Kittens can also hop on Mushroom Trampolines, drop Donut Blocks, and have other skills and though there are many types of kittens in this game, you want to focus on collecting Calico kittens. We'll get to the why, in a moment.

After the main story's completion, Cat Plessie can transport kittens if Mario mounts Cat Plessie while holding a kitten or throws one on top. Convenient? Yes, but there is a danger: if Fury Bowser awakens when you have kittens close by, these kitty minions will turn on Mario and attack even when he's in cat form.

In fact, if Fury Bowser wakes up with Mario holding a kitten, you'll lose your kitty and take damage and if he wakes up while a kitten is on Plessie, it'll teleport the kitten back to where it spawned.

When Mario returns all the Calico kittens to their Oyaneko, he is rewarded a coveted Cat Shine.

OYANEKO

The Oyaneko are three big cats in the Lake Lapcat region, which represent the three Gigabell areas, and they are the sad parents of the lost Calico kittens. They are looking for their kittens and hope they return safely.

One of them is missing a kitten, another three kittens, and the last five kittens.

Your goal is to find the kittens that Oyaneko has lost and carry them back to their parents. If you succeed, you will see it happily reunited with its children instead of weeping, and earn three coins.

PRO TIP: The number of kittens still unaccounted for is shown above the parents' heads. You earn a Cat Shine after returning the last kitten.

PLESSIE/CAT PLESSIE

Plessie's swimming and sliding returns from Mario 3D World in a new role—traveling across island waters. He can also dive and perform a high jump. Plessie is permanently a cat after completing the main story, while Giga Cat Plessie represents a new form of the character that appears after acquiring three Giga Bells.

You have more control over Plessie's movements underwater, which you can use to dodge enemies and propel him forward. Plessie can defeat foes and damage Fury Shadows by simply coming in contact with them if Mario is riding him.

When on land, Plessie can use his tail to attack enemies. He can also deflect green shells, and if invincible Mario is atop when he touches it, he will maintain that status as long as Mario.

PRO TIP: When not riding, Plessie will dive underwater and resurface close to Mario.

ENEMIES

FURY CATS

A Fury Cat is a mysterious version of the Lake Lapcat. When Fury Bowser is active at night in the Bowser's Fury campaign of Super Mario 3D World, all kittens and Oyaneko turn into evil versions of themselves. They look like regular kittens but are now black-furred, red-eyed, and have a purple-red glow with spiky fur!

This posse of kittens turns corrupt every time Fury Bowser starts to rampage. The Fury Cats are inactive until they see you getting close. They'll pounce when they see you and cause damage if they make contact, so try to avoid them at all costs.

PRO TIP: The Fury Cats will slash you, so maintain a safe distance!

When Fury Bowser stops his latest rampage they'll eventually return to normal.

Fury Cats that touch lava, water, Invincible Mario, or White Cat Mario, will disappear and reappear in their previous locations as regular kittens.

These cats can get stunned using the following techniques:

1. Bowser Jr.'s paintbrush
2. Mario's swipe attack
3. Fireballs
4. Boomerangs

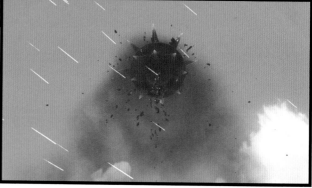

PRO TIP: While they will get stunned temporarily and knocked back, you cannot defeat Fury Cats.

FURY SHADOWS

A Fury Shadow is a Luigi-like creature found in the Bowser's Fury campaign of Super Mario 3D World + Bowser's Fury. They are engulfed in a black slime with red glowing eyes and can move around as Mario does and use the same abilities. They will turn into black balls of sludge, with spikes when hit and then speed off. This enemy has a health bar.

Fury Shadows are on four islands:
1. Fur Step Island
2. Scamper Shores
3. Crisp Climb Castle
4. Risky Whisker Island

They show up on levels titled "Fury Shadow." When you first begin, a Fury Shadow appears, and it bursts out of a spiky blob and starts laughing and running from Mario.

They will follow a predetermined path around the island. You have to chase them and get close enough for Mario or Bowser Jr. to attack with their special moves or catch up while riding Plessie so they can ram into the enemy and take them down. If you do not give chase, it will begin taunting you.

PRO TIP: Defeat them with three hits for a Cat Shine.

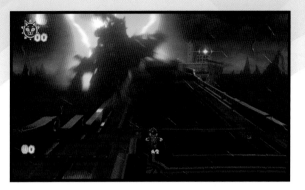

BOSSES

FURY BOWSER

The primary opponent in the Bowser Fury full-campaign of this title is King Bowser Koopa of the Bowser Kingdom. Bowser Jr. was the unintentional artist of that look when he painted Bowser black.

Bowser transforms into a wild and ruthless gigantic kaiju to harm Lapcat Lake in this form. Bowser's complexion turns dark, and he develops luminous features. His hair and the tips of his shell spikes glow red with dazzling luminescent yellow eyes and spikes everywhere. Giga Bells and lighthouses will refer to him as "the beast."

His torso is substantially larger than his head compared with its original form. He has visibly greater pectorals and seems to have a longer tail than other appearances, something he shares alongside its Super Smash Bros. looks.

Fury Bowser will amp up his burning assaults upon adversaries by showering meteorites over an entire area while unleashing extended inferno rays.

His menacing growl is far more terrifying than Bowser's or Dry Bowser's, which are threatening but not as dreadful. Compared to their snarls, Fury Bowser's roar sounds deeper and more sinister, and the reverberating echo makes it even scarier.

PRO TIP: You can witness a different color variant for Fury Bowser! Fury Bowser's orange features will turn a majestic white hue when you accumulate 100 Cat Shines. The effect encompasses his pecs, spikes on his shell, and fur.

Throughout the fight, the vitality gauge will be blue instead of red. However, note that defeating Bowser gets considerably harder once you have collected all 100 Cat Shines. Mario has Bowser Jr.'s help in taking down Fury Bowser in this campaign, and also gets an assist from the Giga Bell.

After he first appears, Fury Bowser shows up at six-minute intervals. He emerges from the fury sun and immediately goes into attack mode.

PRO TIP: To defeat Fury Bowser, you must wait for about 90 seconds for him to stop attacking, or use the Cat Shine power-up to scare him back into hiding.

You also can and should use Giga Bells to challenge Fury Bowser. Since they are of equal size in Giga Cat form, one can directly battle him. You can unlock the Giga Bell to transform into Giga Cat Mario if you've collected enough Cat Shines, and once you do, the fight is on!

Bowser will attack Mario by utilizing his flames, hopping while aiming to ground pound, or burrowing into the surface and releasing spikes. Mario can deal damage to him with a claw swipe or ground-pounding him—a ground pound is possible when Bowser is lying flat on his back.

You can also use Cat Shines to reduce Bowser's vitality before the heavy fighting. If you're able to deplete his reserves enough before the fourth battle, you can skip the rampage and start the final chase sequence.

PRO TIP: While riding on Plessie, you can obtain a Super Bell by passing through Fury Bowser's legs.

During battle, a red vitality bar appears above Fury Bowser. It will drain when he is hit or shocked by a Cat Shine. He will only stay on the field for half of his health during the second and third encounters against him so to beat him, you'll need additional Cat Shines.

It takes six Giga ground pounds to drain his health bar in the initial stage of the game. After enough damage, Bowser will be cast back on the ground, presumably unconscious.

The game displays a different cutscene after the duel depending on your health. Bowser gets up and roars if he has any remaining health before leaving, and he will also begin to glow if his health approaches zero. His glow will brighten until it erupts in a spectacular explosion.

To unlock additional parts of Lake Lapcat, you need to Fight Fury Bowser again. To do that, you need to gather more Cat Shines.

PRO TIP: Fury Bowser's demeanor and the sky's hue will vary as you advance through the game, so be mindful of the mood.

On the first island the skies are dark and Bowser only stays for a few minutes. When you obtain a Cat Shine he will leave immediately.

The sky becomes more reddish in the next area of the campaign, and Bowser will linger much longer. To make him to retreat, you need a Cat Shine or a lighthouse.

In the third stage, the sky becomes an ominous dark crimson, and Bowser will hunker down for much longer. You fight him in this stage—if you've gathered sufficient Cat Shines and trigger a Giga Bell. Also keep in mind that neither the Cat Shines nor lighthouses will be able to fend him off at this point.

In phase two, Bowser will begin to roll to Mario's side and in phase three, he'll unleash a wreath of fireballs, blast spikes at you, and pound the ground relentlessly. You can stun him momentarily by picking up the spikes he launches and hurl them back at him.

GIANT BOWSER

Bowser's Fury mode's last boss is Giant Bowser. After defeating Fury Bowser for the final time, King Bowser Koopa Sr. turns into this enormous form. He will first release the black paint before being consumed in a large explosion. Bowser then emerges from the ocean, massive and enraged. He traps all three Giga Bells in a giant gem.

Giant Bowser attacks with fireballs and fury blasts, while fury spikes are still available to him. To get to the three Giga Bells buried within, Mario must ride Plessie to damage and smash the crystal ball that Giant Bowser is guarding. You do this while avoiding his breath and projectiles.

Bowser gets knocked out after you hit the crystal ball four times. Mario and Plessie use the three bells to make Giant Bowser smaller. They throw him into the sky, causing a spectacular display, and a return of normalcy around Lake Lapcat occurs.

Bowser eventually falls back, shrinking to his original height, thus completing the campaign's primary story line.

ITEMS POWER-UPS

BOOMERANG FLOWER

You are transformed into a Boomerang suit by a white wildflower shaped similar to a boomerang. It features a "V" shaped curvature with a vivid blue stripe running down the end of one side and big eyes. Color-coded boomerangs are available for each usable character.

Your appearance will roughly mimic a standard Boomerang Bro enemy. In comparison to a Boomerang Bro, the colors of your boomerang will get reversed.

PRO TIP: You can obtain a boomerang flower by breaking '?' blocks or beating the Boomerang Bros.

BOOMERANG MARIO

A boomerang suit is a form that allows you to throw a boomerang and strike adversaries. The Boomerang Bro enemy is the inspiration behind the new power-up. Find and grab a Boomerang Flower to get it.

Boomerang Mario can use his boomerang to attack foes, destroy bullets, and grab objects from afar. The advantage of the Boomerang Flower is that it allows you to catch Green Stars and coins from a safe distance. The best time to utilize it is when obtaining Green Stars on top of lava or other hazardous areas.

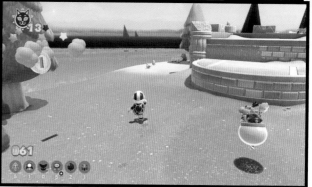

PRO TIP: Mario can avoid being hit by the boomerang by jumping and moving away. If he avoids it successfully, the boomerang will continue on its back-and-forth route until caught.

With each pass, the boomerang's range shrinks. The boomerang will not immediately return to you after the second pass, but will pause for a moment before returning.

If a boomerang collides with a barrier or a wall, you must take a time-out before throwing another. Bullet Bills, Banzai Bills, and opponents that Fire Mario can destroy with his fireballs can be defeated using boomerangs. However, each player can only use one boomerang at a time.

Boomerangs are ideal for boss battles and can come in especially handy if you like to attack from afar. It can also act as a deterrent against enemies who want to meddle with your pals in multiplayer mode.

SUPER BELL

Super Bells are power-up items that grant the Cat Form. They're also called a Cat Bell by some fans. It looks like a bright yellow bell with blended stripes and eyes. Whacking it from a "?" Block produces a whistle paired with a noise animation and gives the character their respective Cat Form.

For example, it gives Mario the ability to scratch or pounce on foes, slide into them, and climb up walls and Goal Poles. The Super Bell also gives increased speed compared to other items. The costume even allows you to ascend on a flagpole and receive one extra life.

You can obtain Super Bells in a few ways:
1. These items typically appear in "?" Blocks, but Cat Goombas also drop them

2. Gathering 100 coins

3. Guiding Plessie below Fury Bowser

4. Ground-pounding a dormant Giga Bell while possessing enough Cat Shines

If you gather all 100 Cat Shines, your cat form will change to match the Giga Cat Form each time you collect any Bell power-up.

PRO TIP: Bowser will transform into Meowser by using a Super Bell. Finally, rather than scaring kittens away, Cat Form will lure them towards you!

CAT MARIO

Cat Mario is a new character making its debut with a new defense and attack move. Cat Mario can climb walls, will cling to structures for a brief moment, can run on all fours, and with an increase in velocity, can claw enemies. He can also perform a diving strike while airborne and attack at various angles. He can claw-swipe or slide at most of his enemies.

PRO TIP: Cat Mario will run sooner than other characters. When he jumps, a jingling or a different jump sound plays.

In Bowser's Fury, the claw dive can now last until it reaches the ground, although it may stop automatically depending on the obstacle. It is also involved in a glitch. The glitch allows using the claw dive while in another form.

One last note: enemies and bosses gain Cat Forms, but they don't gain any extra powers.

FIRE FLOWER

Mario can get this power-up that lets him shoot fireballs to defeat enemies. Other variations include Evil Fire Flower and Ultimate Fire Flower. Fire Flowers are rare because they get replaced by the Super Bell. They are found in Lucky Houses and slot blocks as well.

FIRE MARIO

The Fire Flower power-up from Super Mario Bros. allows Mario to transform into Fire Mario, who can throw fireballs at enemies from a distance.

Fire Mario functions the same as in Super Mario 3D Land while retaining its 2D properties from other games. The fireballs will bounce around and can ricochet off walls. They disappear after a short time, or upon hitting a target.

PRO TIP: Fireballs from Fire Mario can uncover hidden platforms, destroy crates to reveal hidden items and locations, clear the snow on trees, and even destroy mines.

SUPER STAR

You can create a Super Star with an Amiibo scan of any character. The Coin Heavens and Fort Flaptrap regions are the only places with stars in Lake Lapcat. Super Stars in Bowser's Fury have the same mechanics as most other games but only give one extra life with every eighth enemy killed. You can also make other players invincible after touching them with the Super Star power-up activated in multiplayer mode.

INVINCIBLE MARIO

Mario can be invincible for a short time by collecting a Super Star. This item will make Mario run faster and defeat enemies with a touch, though he is not immune to the black goo, falling into deep pits, or taking damage from landscape hazards. If touched by the black goo in Bowser's Fury mode, players will lose invincibility and suffer damage.

⊖ / ⊕ Skip

GIGA BELL

If Mario touches an active Giga Bell, the game will reload into a less detailed map without any objects and transform him into Giga Cat Mario. Giga Bells are items collected by obtaining Cat Shines. They are similar to regular Super Bells but bigger and emit a deep ring and a meow sound.

The black sludge coats the three Giga Bells in their region and will damage you upon touch. Collecting Cat Shines will make Giga Bells usable and help remove goop.

The three regions include:
1. Lakeside — Get the Cat Shine on Fur Step Island
2. Ruins — Defeat Fury Bowser
3. Wasteland — Defeat Fury Bowser three times

Numerous coins appear on top of the pedestal. Once enough Cat Shines have been obtained, the Giga Bells get cleansed and activated. The number of Cat Shines that Mario must collect increases every time you defeat Fury Bowser. If Mario stands in front of the Giga Bell, he can see how many Cat Shines are left to collect.

Once Fury Bowser rises, a cutscene will follow, any available Giga Bells will activate, and when the rampaging ends, the power-up will return to its inactive state. When you get a Giga Bell during a rampage, they instantly become powerful and provide the ability to battle Fury Bowser.

PRO TIP: During Giant Bowser's final battle, he will encase all three Giga Bells in a ball. You must ram Plessie into the encased ball multiple times to break them free.

After you get all three Giga Bells, you finally vanquish Giant Bowser. At the end of the campaign, the Giga Bells are cleansed of goo, allowing Mario to collect them and receive a Super Bell after ground-pounding them from the top.

GIGA CAT MARIO

Giga Cat Mario is a giant form in Bowser's Fury obtained when any three Giga Bells are collected. It is a bigger version of Cat Mario, and his powers increase when he becomes Giga Cat Mario, which changes his fur color and physical features. Giga Cat Mario is like a radiant animal spirit with spiky hair on its head and tail like a lion.

Mario changes into this form to fight Bowser. Once Mario comes into contact with the Giga Bell, the HUD disappears, and a battle with Fury Bowser begins.

After you collect enough Cat Shines, they will remove the corruption on the Giga Bells and allow you to use them while Bowser is on his rampage.

PRO TIP: Giga Cat Mario has the same attributes as Cat Mario, but he loses some moves and can't climb as well. He is however invulnerable to the black sludge.

Giga Cat Moves:
1. Crouch
2. Dash
3. Ground Pound Jump
4. Long Jump
5. Roll

Giga Cat Attacks:
1. Claw Swipe
2. Claw Dive

Remember that although big, he is not invincible. Giga Cat will take damage from lava and Fury Bowser's attacks, and loses a size increase every time he gets hurt. If Mario takes damage from Bowser and is defeated, he can collect a Giga Bell close to the respawn point to restart the battle quickly.

You can transform into Giga Cat with a power-up an unlimited number of times. If you have collected a Giga Bell in any region to fight Fury Bowser, it won't show up during the battle but it will reappear eventually, notifying you with a distinct sound alert.

GIGA CAT PLESSIE

After the final battle with Giant Bowser, Plessie obtains all three Giga Bells and transforms into a gigantic cat version. Giga Cat Plessie grows to an immense size and can tackle Giant Bowser, knocking him out of sight.

PRO TIP: Giga Cat Plessie returns to original size and stays as a cat on future saves at the restart of the game.

CAT SHINE!
Key to the Cat Shine

LUCKY BELL/LUCKY CAT POWER-UP

The Lucky Bell is a power-up that turns Mario into a Lucky Cat with a bell collar. It looks like a brown jingle bell or acorn with eyes. The Lucky Bell serves as an upgrade to the Super Bell and starts showing up in World Mushroom-2.

Lucky Cat Mario

The Lucky Cat Mario is a creature form obtained when performing a ground pound after grabbing the Lucky Bell. It resembles the Mario Cat form, and is also known as Golden Statue Mario or Maneki-Neko Mario.

Mario can turn into a Lucky Cat for 12 seconds, during which time he experiences invincibility and earns coins when falling in this form. In fact, the higher the fall, the more coins he collects!

Mario will revert to his original self if he stops stomping. He can defeat his enemies in one hit without getting hurt, such as Spike Bars and Fuzzies.

This power-up is ultimately very similar to the Tanooki Statue form, and it cannot protect against lava or crushing. It also prevents you from doing midair rolls.

SUPER LEAF

Super Leafs return in Super Mario 3D World but show-up more sparingly. Super Leafs start appearing after World three and give the same Tanooki form as in Super Mario 3D Land.

It is a brown leaf that turns Mario into a Tanooki/raccoon and gives him the ability to glide through the air for a short time and attack enemies with his tail.

Tanooki Mario

In Bowser's Fury, you can be a regular or White Tanooki. Most of the Tanooki suits in this game remain unchanged from 3D Land when transformed, and Rosalina's is similar to Peach's.

PRO TIP: Tanooki Mario is an alternate form of our favorite plumber that can still tail-whip enemies, even when underwater!

You get a Tanooki suit when you obtain a Super Leaf. The mechanics are different from Super Mario Bros. 3 because in this game you can only glide instead of having the ability to fly, though you can speed-up or slow down your descent.

Mario's move set has changed with the introduction of tail spin, allowing him to tail whip continuously while stationary or moving. He can spin his tail for quick ascents.

INVINCIBILITY BELL

The Invincibility Bell is a power-up obtained by scanning the Cat Mario or Cat Peach Amiibo. The Mario Amiibo is guaranteed to produce one, but the Peach Amiibo has a lower spawn success and instead has the chance to generate other power-ups. The design is like the Super Bell but with white stripes on the front and back.

PRO TIP: The Invincibility Bell will turn into a Super Bell if sent to storage.

White Cat Mario

White Cat Mario is the white, sparkly version of Cat Mario who has Cat Mario's abilities and White Tanooki's invincibility against enemies and obstacles, similar to how the Invincibility Leaf provides Super Leaf abilities and invincibility.

PRO TIP: You can become White Cat Mario by acquiring an Invincibility Bell.

You're able to enjoy white cat form until you lose a life or complete the level, or you can change while you're in white cat form with any power-up—but only in Bowser's Fury campaign.

White Cat Mario will turn back to Super Mario if he touches the black slime, and you can make contact with Fury Bowser when invincible.

INVINCIBILITY LEAF/ GOLD LEAF/INVINCIBLE SUPER LEAF

The Invincibility Leaf is a gold and white-colored power-up that gives you permanent invulnerability. The Gold Leaf in Bowser's Fury has the same effects as in other Mario games but is now available for carrying in your item storage.

PRO TIP: Be sure to use Invincibility Leaves promptly since they will turn into Super Leaves if you lose a life or finish the level.

White Tanooki Mario

A White Tanooki Suit is a power-up that endows you with the effects of a Raccoon/ Tanooki Suit and Starman but with limitations. You gain the same abilities from the Tanooki Suit but don't receive every power of Starman,

such as increased speed and jump velocity or added points from defeating enemies. Like the Starman, it also does not protect against landscape hazards, including:

- Lava
- Ink
- Poison Waters
- Long Falls

White Tanooki Mario appears after five lost lives, but the number of lives that need to be lost to use this power in multiplayer mode is different. When you get the Invincible Super Leaf, you will turn into White Tanooki.

When you play through the game with White Tanooki Mario, completion stars lose their shine, and the level's score remains at zero. However, a second play-through without using this form restores the stars' shine, saves score-count updates on your game file, and removes the Assist Block.

PRO TIP: Though dynamic, this suit is vulnerable to the black sludge and is not available on Champion's Road.

This walkthrough should provide more than an ample head start into this deep and diverse Mario game, but we don't want to spoil everything. With this guide, you should have all the basic tools and techniques you need to know to defuse and defeat Bowser's Fury!

ALSO AVAILABLE
WHEREVER BOOKS ARE SOLD

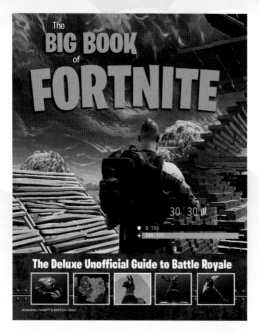

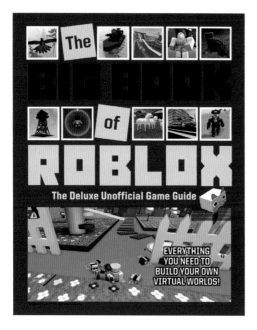

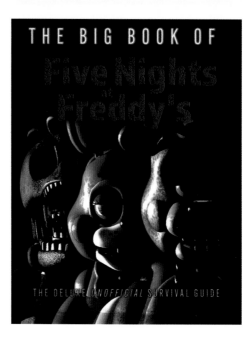

AND AT WWW.TRIUMPHBOOKS.COM/GAMING

TRIUMPH
B O O K S

TRIUMPHBOOKS.COM
@TRIUMPHBOOKS